GARDENDESIGNDETAILS

GARDENDESIGNDETAILS

arne maynard with anne de verteuil

HARPER
DESIGN
international

An imprint of HarperCollins*Publishers*

GARDEN DESIGN DETAILS

Text copyright © 2004 by Arne Maynard
Book design and layout copyright © 2004
by Conran Octopus Limited

HarperCollins books may be purchased for educational,
business, or sales promotional use. For information,
please write: Special Markets Department,
HarperCollins*Publishers*,
10 East 53rd Street, New York, NY 10022.

First published in the United States in 2004 by:
Harper Design International

Published in the United States by:
Collins Design
An Imprint of HarperCollins*Publishers*
10 East 53rd Street, New York, NY 10022
collinsdesign@harpercollins.com
www.harpercollins.com

First published in the United Kingdom in 2004 by:
Conran Octopus Limited
a part of Octopus Publishing Group
2–4 Heron Quays, London E14 4JP
www.conran-octopus.co.uk

Distributed throughout North America by:
HarperCollins*Publishers*
10 East 53rd Street, New York, NY 10022
Fax: (212) 207-7654

Library of Congress Control Number: 2004100438

ISBN-10: 0-06-059631-7
ISBN-13: 978-0-06-059631-6

Printed in China
Second Printing, 2006

CONTENTS

INTRODUCTION

RIGHT Emphatic planting is used to great effect in this garden. Olive trees define the strong vertical elements within the garden and contrast in perfect harmony with the soft horizontal planting below.

BELOW The lead capping on a plain oak post protects and, at the same time, adds detail and decoration to the structure.

THIS BOOK IS AN INSPIRATIONAL PORTFOLIO OF IDEAS AND IMAGES THAT will help open your mind to some of the many different ways of interpreting a garden. Its aim is to show that imaginative, exciting and often unexpectedly successful results can be achieved by trying different effects – perhaps the way you clip or shape a hedge, the pointing style of a garden wall, or simply how you mow the lawn. The idea is to free ourselves from set ways of doing things and, instead, to consider alternative techniques.

The main part of the book looks at the fixed structures that make up the garden framework, including walls, fences, terraces, paths, lawns, edging details and garden buildings. For ease of use, these structures are divided into three separate sections: Verticals, Horizontals and Punctuation. These are the terms that describe their visual and dynamic function within the space. Wherever a garden is in the world, it is composed of these same three elements. The horizontals and verticals make up the garden space, with its flat expanses of grass and paving, and its defining upright boundaries, trees and levels. Punctuation, in the form of garden ornament, water features, seating areas and garden buildings, adds vitality and purpose to the design. The balancing act between the horizontals, verticals and punctuation is what gives a garden its particular dynamic.

Although the book does not cover soft planting (the herbaceous and seasonal flowering shrubs), it does look at ways of using walls, hedges and edges that define those spaces, and which will later be filled in with seasonal colour and texture.

The final part of the book, Casework, features eight gardens by different designers, including some of my own designs, one of which is currently in progress. These gardens illustrate how the verticals, horizontals and punctuation have been put together to create a particular kind of space.

BELOW Sited at the bend of a river, this intriguing grass mound has breathtaking views in all directions. A wicker seat built into a cavity on one side of the mound takes advantage of these views, while remaining a cosy and secluded hiding-place from the world.

BELOW The fence that this
gate would normally sit in has
become obsolete, and the
knotted old espaliered fruit trees
now perform its role.

In one garden, the horizontal plane may dominate because of the surrounding landscape; in another, where space on the horizontal plane is limited, there may be many contrasting vertical elements. In all cases, there will be a satisfying balance between the two and always some form of punctuation to give a rhythm to the whole.

Garden Design Details is not intended as a comprehensive list of garden elements, nor as an instruction manual, but rather as an exhortation to open up the imagination to the endless possibilities for variation. It hopes to encourage the reader to invent his or her own solutions, using the materials and resources at hand. Some of the garden structures illustrated here have undoubtedly cost a great deal of money, but there are as many equally stunning examples of skill and ingenuity that have cost nothing more than time and the willingness to experiment.

LEFT These cleft and weathered pieces of timber create a casual and transparent boundary around the edges of an informal garden.

BELOW This wall has been constructed from knapped flints, the colour and pattern creating a rich and textural vernacular detail.

There seems to be a synchronicity in the way ideas and fashions spread, and quite often it will happen that designers or gardeners use similar themes or motifs at the same time as each other. The plain fact is that, just as in every other sphere, there is nothing new in garden design; it has all been done before. One of the very best ways to find fresh ideas is to be continually on the lookout for them. When you visit gardens or walk in the countryside, observe, take photos, make sketches, look at wall details, gate latches, the way a path travels, how a border is edged. Don't be afraid to do this, there is nothing wrong in borrowing ideas – they are, after all, common currency. It is your particular interpretation applied to your own set of circumstances that will make the result unique.

verticals

ABOVE It can be exciting to layer verticals one in front of the other, setting off the contrasts in plant species. Cutting the layers differently helps to create sculptural flow and movement.

ABOVE CENTRE A strong vertical opening within this yew hedge frames the view and the simple iron gate perfectly, allowing a visual connection between the garden and surrounding landscape.

The elements that create vertical height within a garden are its walls, hedges, fences, steps, level changes, entrances and openings; in larger gardens, height may also be provided by topiary trees, allées, tunnels and groupings of trees, such as orchards. The purpose of this section of the book is to act as a springboard for the imagination and look at the many ways in which these elements can be interpreted. Convention tends to make us think along prescribed lines, but a wall, for example, need not be straight nor need it just be made of brick; the shape and form of a hedge can be altered dramatically by clipping it in a different way, say, by giving it a wavy or castellated top. Many everyday structures can be made into beautiful and original features by paying attention to their detailing: incorporating a small pebble mosaic into a path, making an intricate carved panel for a plain timber door or planting the crevices in a flight of steps with aromatic thymes.

Vertical structures have several roles to play within the garden space, the principal one being enclosure. This may be enclosure of the whole space, or division of the garden into a series of separate spaces or garden rooms. These divisions bring an important sense of proportion into the garden, helping relate the space to a human scale. The individual areas can be used for different purposes and given distinctive characters: kitchen garden, herb garden, flower garden and so on.

The divisions themselves may be walls, hedges, allées or trees and, according to context, may be used in a variety of ways. Hedges that are allowed to grow tall will screen out unwanted views; if they are kept low, they will permit views. A line of pleached trees may be used as a formal hedge on stilts, allowing glimpses out between their trunks. Where something unobtrusive is needed, the division may be transparent or semi-transparent; although railings and picket fences create physical barriers, they invite you to look though at what lies on the other side.

Verticals offer great opportunities for creating drama within the garden. They can be used to announce a change of direction or, placed like signposts, they can guide the visitor through the garden. An entrance through a wall or hedge that is flanked by a pair of topiary trees gains an element of significance and tells you something about what you may expect to find on the other side. A plain wooden door suggests mystery and a secret yet to be revealed.

Perhaps the greatest potential for vertical impact is that offered by steps and terracing in a sloping garden. In addition to their obvious practical function, these junctions at the changes of levels can be made into wonderful stages for movement, viewing and looking ahead and behind over the route you have just taken.

ABOVE An ingenious use of sawn timber creates an organic boundary between the garden and the woodland beyond, as well as the perfect structure for roses and honeysuckle to scramble over.

An ancient yew hedge is given additional vertical punctuation by the topiary domes growing out of its castellated top.

The unusual direction in which the stones have been laid give this traditional dry-stone wall a fresh, more contemporary appearance.

Pattern in brick walling can be introduced in a number of different ways. Here, bricks have been left out at regular intervals to create a chequerboard effect, with plants tumbling out through the gaps.

There are many different mortars and finishes that can be used for building walls. In this traditional stone wall, small pieces of stone have been pushed into the wet lime mortar joints to create a striking vernacular detail.

Randomly placed yew topiary give this garden the vertical height and scale needed to complement the woodland and hills in the distance.

Trelliswork does not always have to be made of sawn timber. Here, living willow has been twisted and woven together to form a beautiful green, and eventually gnarled, semi-transparent structure – perfect for making a simple division within the garden.

HEDGES, WALLS, TRANSPARENTS

Earth and cob walls stem from antiquity and are among the simplest and earliest forms of construction. Beautifully executed with sharp angles, this ancient technique is rejuvenated here as a very contemporary wall.

Trelliswork can be made in a variety of patterns, with the timber painted or left bare. Painted timber, as shown here, with a star-shaped pattern cut into the wood, suits a more formal location.

Low and casually clipped lavender hedges form wave-like structures, giving an informal and contemporary feel to this garden.

HEDGES

VERSATILE AND HIGHLY AFFORDABLE, HEDGES PERFORM
a similar role to walls, but they create an environment
that is altogether softer. A wide variety of plants can
be used to make boundaries and divisions within the
garden and each has its own distinctive characteristics.
A yew hedge, for example, kept tall and precisely
clipped, makes a barrier with the formality and
strength of a garden wall. On the other hand, field
maple (*Acer campestre*), cut like a field hedge with
a rounded top and organic, flowing lines, makes a
gentle, informal division.

The flexibility of hedging extends to the way in
which it can be adapted over a period of time. You
can completely change the pattern of a hedge by
altering the way it is cut: initially, it might be quite
formal, then perhaps, as time passes and the garden
develops, you might decide that it needs to be less
dominant. You could reduce the height, or cut the top
so that it is wavy. If a new building obscures a view
from the garden, an existing hedge could be allowed
to grow higher to become a screen.

A hedge made from a single plant variety will have
a tendency to look formal. Mixing varieties, say, box
(*Buxus sempervirens*) with yew (*Taxus baccata*), or box
with beech (*Fagus sylvatica*), creates a tapestry hedge
that has variety and a greater textural quality. In a city
garden, a wild-looking native hedge might be used to
make an unexpected contrast with the surrounding
buildings. A favourite combination of mine, and one
that I use frequently as a hedge for kitchen gardens, is
hornbeam (*Carpinus betulus*) and crab apple (*Malus*).
By allowing the crab apples to flower and the fruit to
set, the hedge will contain the essence of an apple
orchard in spring and summer. Then, in autumn, the

bronzy leaves of the hornbeam will mix with the red
or yellow fruits that hang on the hedge into winter.

Hedges don't necessarily have to be evergreen – the
subtle winter tracery of bare branches can be a lovely
feature in its own right. Field maple, with its close-
knit and cinnamon-brown branches, is a gorgeous
sight in winter. Even without leaves, the density of the
network of branches holds the eye and has the effect
of dissolving the view beyond.

By mixing varieties imaginatively, it is possible to
use a plant's strengths to disguise its weaknesses.

ABOVE Certain plants, such as
rosemary and lavender, are not
suitable for clipping into rigid
square hedges. Their natural
growth habit and shape need to
be worked with to bring out their
own free-form qualities.

ABOVE Over a period of time, previously formal clipped hedges take on a marvellous informal shape. It is possible to clip new hedges to mimic this look, helping to bring an immediate feeling of maturity to a new garden.

As a garden shrub, the winter-flowering honeysuckle, (*Lonicera purpusii*) can be rather messy, but its flowers have a lovely fragrance. When planted with hornbeam, it makes a superb hedge for bordering a path, which, in January and February, becomes a heavenly scented walkway.

Familiarity makes things invisible over time. Using known materials in a new and fresh way allows us to see them as if for the first time. Edges and small internal divisions within the garden are usually made with low-growing plants like lavender and dwarf box (*B. sempervirens* 'Suffruticosa'), but you could use large hedging plants instead and keep them cut small. Beech, for instance, can be made to form a wonderful low hedge no more than 14in (35cm) high, provided it is clipped frequently. In hot climates, myrtle (*Myrtus communis*) and olive (*Olea europaea*) can be used in the same way. Similarly, hawthorn (*Crataegus monogyna*), traditionally grown as a big country hedge, might instead be used as an attractive low hedge in a medieval knot garden, giving the design a kind of naivety that looks modern just because it offers a surprise.

The trick with using potentially large plants as low hedging is to look at them and ask yourself if they can be kept small. You need to be open-minded enough to experiment and take the approach that if it doesn't work, it can be changed. The whole gardening process is one of change, and if something proves to be too difficult, then it can be altered. After all, the willingness to experiment is a large part of what makes gardening enjoyable.

A beautiful striped hedge made from alternating 1.8m (6ft) runs of yew and beech could be a stimulating solution for a garden with a contemporary feel. To keep the 'joins' looking crisp and sharp, a 6mm (⅛in) steel plate, allowing it to go rusty, can be fixed between the sections, keeping the plants close but distinct from one another. You could carry the same idea further into the garden by creating a chequer-board pattern with a knot garden made of dwarf box and hawthorn.

There are countless ways in which a hedge can have its character altered by cutting. The top may be kept flat or clipped into rolling curves. The sides may be vertical or sloping, and the angle of the slope may be used to create wedge shapes that are alternated with square-cut blocks like vertical buttresses. Where a run of hedge is interrupted to make an entrance into another part of the garden, added definition can be given by cutting the hedge into pillars on either side of the gap or bringing them together to form an arch. A pair of yew piers might have topiary finials clipped into the top of them to give the impression of extra weight and grandeur.

Hedges don't need to go from one point to another in a simple straight line. The line can be serpentine, zig-zag, castellated, or it can form a strong contemporary pattern on the ground. Nor do hedges need to be the same height all the way along their length: one section of a hedge could be made to curve down into the garden, forming a spiral like a green sculpture. Inside the spiral, the hedge might have a narrow slit cut into one side at eye level, focusing on an urn in the distance or the beautiful bark of a tree trunk. Hedges can also be used to redirect and even disorientate. Arranged maze-like, hedges may conceal an enclosure with an urn or small pool; the exit from the maze could send you off in a completely different direction.

ABOVE The serpentine form of this yew hedge creates a fluid division, allowing light and shadows to bring further interest to the vertical structure. The shape is echoed in the mown grass path that runs alongside it.

FAR LEFT This boundary hedge of beech forms a powerful vertical element that is strong enough to sit comfortably with the large beech trees behind.

There are many fascinating ways of manipulating plants for particular purposes and effects, which, when done well, show off the particular skill of the gardener. Traditional hedge laying – the method used for stock-proofing – creates a strongly patterned, fence-like structure that gives an age-old quality to a garden boundary. Laying involves cutting halfway through the trunks of the vertical growth of the hedge and laying them down almost horizontally at an angle of 30 degrees. Hazel rods are inserted at intervals and the top is woven together. As with coppicing, the new growth shoots up from the base. Traditional materials would be sloe (*Prunus spinosa*), hawthorn and hazel (*Corylus avellana*). A modern twist on this traditional technique would be to lay the plants at 45 degrees, supported on canes, and have them form a lattice of interlacing stems, the skeleton of which is hidden behind leaves in summer but then emerges in winter to add a fresh element of interest to the garden.

A Cornish wall – half-wall, half-hedge – could be used to introduce an aged quality, or to give instant height. In a new garden, a native hedge planted on

LEFT Traditional layered hedges don't always need to have an agricultural context. They can be adapted and used in both traditional and modern garden designs.

RIGHT Our everyday environment can be a tremendous source of inspiration. The way these hedges flow down the hill, following the contours, could trigger many design ideas for your own garden.

RIGHT A box hedge has been clipped to form a number of interlocking balls, creating a sculpted texture, which acts as a wonderful foil for frost and snow in winter. The play of light and shadow across the hedge adds an element of drama.

an earth mound, or a grass bank underplanted with wild flowers would bring both height and apparent maturity. The simple device of making the same bank more sharply angled and geometric achieves a look that is crisp and contemporary.

Where a solid barrier is not needed, attractive internal divisions can be made with espaliered or cordoned fruit trees, perhaps between a vegetable garden and an herbaceous border, or as a productive division for a town garden, giving flowers and fruit but taking up minimal space. Pleached trees can also be used to make garden rooms and enclosures. In a town garden, a small vegetable plot might be kept separate and, at the same time, given wind protection by a pleached hedge set in a path of chippings.

Pleached trees are essentially hedges on stilts. The exposed trunks allow views and movement, so the effect is less overwhelming than a full hedge. A wide range of plants can be pleached, from the traditional hornbeam and lime (*Tilia cordata*) to olive and the Judas tree (*Cercis siliquastrum*). Whitebeam (*Sorbus aria*) also makes an excellent pleached hedge, and its silver felty leaves look particularly good in conjunction with lavenders and other greys and silvers.

Crab apple, hawthorn, holm oak (*Quercus ilex*) and pear trees all pleach well, each one producing a completely different mood and emphasis. You can employ the visual shock of training informal plants in a formal way to create something that is new and interesting. A hedge of pleached crab apples creates an orchard in the flat plane that looks particularly striking in winter, when, with the fruit still hanging from its bare branches, it is seen against a line of evergreens or a dark wall.

WALLS

BELOW LEFT Walls need not always be made of brick. Here, a tall earth wall covered in grass encircles the garden, protecting it from the external environment and embracing the setting outside its confines.

BELOW CENTRE This modern rendered wall creates a simple but very strong boundary within the garden, allowing the plants in the foreground to become the key players.

WALLS ARE THE DOMINANT VERTICAL ELEMENTS IN A garden. Generally built from brick or stone, they may be used to form a perimeter boundary that acts as the protective outer skin of the garden. Within larger gardens, walls may be used internally to create protected areas, such as a kitchen garden, and the walls themselves become warmth-retaining structures on which fruit and tender climbers can be trained.

Brick walling is one of the most versatile options for vertical structures, and the small 'units' create pattern within the garden. Curves and circles are easily accommodated with brick, and walls can be built in a wide variety of different bonds, including Dutch, Flemish, English Garden and rat-trap. A skilled bricklayer can change the height of a wall gracefully and fluidly wherever necessary along its length. The fact that a wall can be built to a height of 3m (10ft) or more makes brick a good choice where height is needed. But it is important that all but the very lowest wall should be more than one brick thick. Thin walls look mean and are unstable; they also undermine the sense of solid permanence that a wall should give.

A long run of brick walling can be interrupted for added interest. A pair of brick pillars flanking an entrance, for instance, could be given a rectangular insert of small pebbles or peg tiles in a herringbone pattern. The capping of a wall is also an important detail that can be used to give the wall a particular

look or style. Stone capping or curved, half-octagon and other pre-shaped brick cappings are traditional finishes, but a new brick wall could be given a contemporary look with a thick oak plank laid directly over the final soldier course and left to weather. In the right setting, a planted capping can be beautiful. A low brick wall with a shallow trough of soil in the top can be planted with prostrate thymes or sedums; the same idea can be applied to pillars, with low brick upstands making a planting space for sedums or sempervivums. The joints can be finished in a variety of ways; my personal preference is for a mix of lime mortar and gritty sand that's struck off level with the brick, then gently brushed off to give a lovely textured finish.

In modern gardens, brick can be used simply to create an uncluttered effect. There is a virtually unlimited choice of bricks, and the smooth, even metallic-looking finishes can be used successfully in contemporary settings. Alternatively, walls cast from concrete create a clean profile and are perfect where crisp, angular, painted walls are required.

Brick has strong associations with Victorian and Georgian period buildings, whereas a mortared stone wall made with large, crisp blocks of limestone makes a very contemporary-looking structure. The colour of the stone can be pale; a rich red sandstone can be the colour of cinnamon. Varying the texture within the wall adds interest, and a wall of clean, sawn stone could

BELOW A glass wall with a surface of running water introduces an element of mystery as to what might lie on the other side. Once the water is turned off, the garden beyond is revealed.

have a band of chiselled stone running through it, or a base and capping made of rusticated stone. Stone is an expensive material and long runs of stone walling are very costly, but a section of wall measuring 3 x 2.5m (10 x 8ft), for example, could be used as a semi-division across a long narrow garden. The stones should be closely butted up with the minimum of jointing; if a path runs either side of the wall, its tactile qualities will be fully appreciated. You could even carve a pattern or motif into it, so that it becomes a work of art in its own right.

Dry-stone walls are made without mortar joints by arranging the stones one on top of the other, and are best as low walls, 1–1.2m (3–4ft) high. Taller walls can be built with mortared joints to imitate dry-stone walls. With their strong sense of place, dry-stone walls should be used where they belong in the landscape.

Dry-stone walling can be used to make fluid sweeps and curves, like sculptor Andy Goldsworthy's wall in Grizedale Forest, Cumbria, which meanders around the trunks of trees on its journey. Planted with thymes and lavenders in the crevices or, in a cool shady situation with ferns and mosses, a section of dry-stone wall becomes a living tapestry that could be imported into a city garden as a beautiful internal division or even made into a small maze or labyrinth planted with thymes and sedums.

In areas without natural reserves of stone or clay for brick-making, the traditional cob wall was made by piling any materials that could be found to hand – chalk, soil, straw – into layers between shuttering, and then compacting them. The resulting rammed-earth wall is wide and chunky, and can be built up to great heights for walls and buildings, then plastered

TOP LEFT There are dozens of ways to build walls using recycled materials. This temporary wall has been made from old roof tiles, but it could equally well have been built from slabs of stone paving.

TOP RIGHT Log walls are simple and easy to construct, and could be made from recycled wood. If this wall were capped with turf, wild flowers and grasses would flourish on top.

RIGHT The largest stones in this wall have been positioned first to form the main bulk of the wall. Smaller pieces then fill the gaps, allowing light to filter through between the stones and giving the structure a weightlessness that it would otherwise not possess.

over with lime plaster. A cob wall must have capping to protect it from the weather, and traditional forms include thatched stone coping and tiled tops. Made crisp and sharp and painted a strong earth colour, a cob wall can be an excellent way of bringing a modern element into a garden, while still holding hands with its ancient origins.

Earth walls and turf walls make beautiful, subtle and organic divisions either within a garden or at a woodland edge. The earth is usually mounded up into a circle to give the wall strength; a beautiful kitchen garden could be created within a series of concentric earth wall circles, with perhaps a cherry orchard planted outside for protection. The walls might be built up to a height of 1m (3ft) and planted with thymes and lavenders or prostrate rosemary. There is something profoundly spiritual about these spaces, and there is an energy within them that would be perfect for growing vegetables and herbs.

Some earth walls are topped with turf, but the usual method for making turf walls is to pile old turves, one on top of the other, to the required height, then drape

new turf on top and peg it in. In sunny and warm-climate gardens, a sedum wall could be made by pegging ready-grown sedum mats on top instead. In a shady garden, the wall could be covered with galvanized poultry wire to hold it in place and planted up with ivy. Or a turf wall might be a division in an open space, covered in wild flowers.

Stacked logs, split or left whole make attractive temporary walls that become colonized by mosses and ferns as they decompose, eventually leaving a very fertile little area of ground. (Archaeologists have detected traces of old walls like this.) A log wall could be used in a town garden to make a division that leads into a shady area at the far end. The addition of a pair of sawn timber posts and an

LEFT A dry-stone wall is the perfect place for self-seeding plants to establish. This wall, baked in the sun, has been colonized with aubrieta.

entrance with a gate will make it look like a wall, rather than a pile of logs. Already you will have a sense of the kind of space you are moving into, where there may be cardiocrinums and white species peonies with hazels. Nothing could be simpler to build: no foundations are needed and if you want to change its position, you can simply unstack and rebuild it.

Straw-bale walling is another form of construction that's both fun and environmentally friendly; it would be a wonderful way to create heat-retaining walls for a kitchen garden. The blocks are built up to the required height on footings and pegged together with stakes. They can be shaped with a chainsaw and then plastered over with lime-plaster, like a cob wall, and capped to protect it from weathering.

LEFT The environment in which a wall is built changes its character over time. This rough stone wall in the shade of large trees has become encrusted with a thick and velvety cloak of moss.

RIGHT This low brick wall supports and complements the informal planting that tumbles over its top and seems to greet the plants below.

LEFT A simple and elegant vertical division within a garden setting has been given added interest by varying the height of the wooden posts and painting them in a range of complementary earth colours.

TRANSPARENTS

THE PICKET, OR PALING, FENCE IS THE PERFECT EXAMPLE of a semi-transparent or see-through vertical. Traditionally made of wood and most often used along the outer boundary of a garden, in its most basic form it is a row of timber frames on which can be fixed either simple or elaborately patterned sawn uprights (the pickets, or palings). It is one of the most adaptable types of fencing, and offers an economical way of creating a barrier. It allows light through, plants can spill between the pickets, and climbers can be trained over it. It may be painted or left as natural wood.

Picket fencing is not at all difficult to make, and there are countless ways of adapting it to suit different situations. Even apparently small changes, such as altering the thickness or the width of the uprights, will have an effect on the overall look of the fence.

A plain fence could be made using flat sections of planking for the verticals with divisions at intervals made by posts with a carefully detailed capping. For a design adapted to a more formal situation, you might choose to use square section palings that are like iron railings instead.

A totally individual picket fence might be composed purely of beautiful pieces of driftwood nailed to a horizontal frame and then painted with a lime wash. An informal country fence could be made up of wobbly hazel rods or finger-thick coppiced branches with the bark left on. The fencing material may be shaped entirely by nature or carefully turned by man or machine, but however grand or simple the design, what chiefly matters is that the materials themselves should be beautiful.

LEFT A country-crafted wooden picket fence, which follows the curve of the boundary, has been made to resemble formal and more expensive traditional iron railings.

LEFT This sheet metal fence has been constructed in such a way that when looked at straight on it is possible to see through to the garden. However, when viewed along its length, it acts as a screen, while still allowing sunlight to filter through.

Fencing introduces an important element of pattern into the garden, from a fence made of living willow woven into diamonds to an intricate trelliswork design. If it is not overdone, mixing sections of different fencing materials can be an extremely effective way of setting up some interesting variations on pattern within the garden. A fence composed of alternating and contrasting panels could be used to establish a strong rhythmic pattern that fits in well with a contemporary design. The panels might swap between natural and sawn timbers, square-cut posts and round poles, vertical posts and horizontal bars, or even smooth planed timber and natural wood still covered with bark.

For extra height, trelliswork is often fixed to the top of a wall. Trellis panels can be made up in a variety of patterns, from squares or diamonds to diagonals, and using a diverse range of materials. A trellis might be something formal, elegant and elaborate made of sawn timber and beautifully painted, or it might be free-form and organic, composed of a wonderful assortment of pieces of wood and driftwood, lashed together with copper wire or twine.

Another type of beautiful fence can be made from split chestnut palings nailed to wooden horizontals. Again, these materials are inexpensive and no special skills are required to construct the fence. The palings can be left raw, limewashed, painted with exterior paint or sand-blasted to bring out the silvery grain of the wood. Personally, I don't like the effect of wood-stains and prefer the kind of opaque finish achieved by limewashing or conventional paint. For this type of fence, you can also paint straight onto

rough wood, perhaps using only a thin layer of paint, so that the grain of the wood still shows through.

Each variation in fence design – its height and the way in which the panels align at the top, whether straight, scalloped or dropping down in a curve to a gate – creates something new and different. By putting skill and imagination to work on these natural materials, we can create as many different interpretations as there are gardens.

Metal railings offer another and more transparent form of division, which is both elegant and visually non-invasive. Estate railings – narrow iron rails that run horizontally – can be used to make a subtle sub-division within a garden. Classic cast-iron railings

make an elegant boundary for town-house frontages, and, although expensive, can be very effectively reinterpreted to give a modern look.

Stone balustrading is a formal architectural device and one of the more expensive forms of semi-transparent vertical barrier. There are hundreds of different styles, ranging from the highly ornate to the simplest form of undecorated, square stone columns fixed between stone pediment and capping, and looking like a ladder on its side. Balustrading is probably best used in short runs – at a level change, by steps or at the edge of terracing, where a physical barrier is needed. An alternative version for an old Tudor house might be turned green oak posts finished with carved finials.

ABOVE LEFT This home-made division has been cut from within the garden and woven together to make a simple but beautiful organic fence.

ABOVE CENTRE The estate railing – one of my favourite forms of fencing – can be used in both formal and contemporary settings, and as a boundary to a garden, where it allows nature to grow through at its feet.

LEFT Wreathed in early morning winter mist in this most romantic of settings, mossed and mellow stone balustrading adorns a landing stage of flagstones that opens onto the river.

Entrances need not be rectangular. This moon gate within a garden pavilion lures the visitor into a mysterious new world beyond.

In a woodland garden, stone or brick steps would be incongruous, but these large tree-trunk slabs wedged in the soil form a natural and seductive staircase.

Sound is an important consideration when choosing materials for entrances or openings. The sharp click of a latch lifting on a metal gate or door creates a very different atmosphere from the dull sound of a latch on a wooden gate or door.

Decorative as well as functional, this simple home-made gateway prevents wild animals entering and feasting in the vegetable garden.

In a steeply sloping garden, one of the first and most important design steps to make is to create level terraces. Here, this has been achieved with a series of dry-stone retaining walls.

ENTRANCES AND OPENINGS, LEVEL CHANGES, STEPS

The clean, sharp treads of these stone steps have been softened by *Erigeron karvinskianus*, which has been allowed to self-seed along the edges.

A simple and enticing entrance through a beech hedge invites the visitor to view the internal vault-like structure of its branches and explore the garden beyond.

ENTRANCES AND OPENINGS

ENTRANCES AND OPENINGS PLAY AN IMPORTANT ROLE IN the vocabulary of garden design. Naturally, they have a practical function, but they also have great potential for creating a sense of theatre in the garden. With well-chosen dressing-up or down, they mark the 'arrival points', of which there may be one or many, and create atmosphere at each transition from one part of the garden to another. Entrances and openings can also be viewed as punctuation points – sometimes a question mark as to what lies behind, or a comma as you pause before walking through a gap in a wall.

Doorways in walls are usually rectangular, but they can equally well be oval or square, even leaf-shaped or circular. A moon gate – a circular aperture cut out of the wall – is a feature that you, literally, have to step over and through, and this act brings with it the magical suggestion of entering another world.

There is something satisfying about a gate or a door at the threshold between one environment and another. The act of having to turn a handle and physically push the door open reinforces the ceremonial of arriving or departing. On arriving, you open the door into another world, a secret garden, and when you leave, you close the door behind you to keep it safe.

Solid barriers and doors make definite statements about enclosure and privacy. A solid gate set into a large, high wall creates an element of mystery about what lies on the other side. Occasionally, wooden doors have a small metal grille at eye level. There are situations when a door or gate would create too strong a division within the garden, and it is best simply to leave an opening that can be 'dressed'. So, an opening cut into the vertical division – the

ABOVE Openings need not always have a door or gate. A gothic arch cut into this wall has been framed and given added importance by the deceptively casual way in which the vine follows its contours.

ABOVE A pile of logs over a simple crooked arch forms a sylvan entrance into an unknown, possibly magical world beyond. In time, the logs will be clothed with ferns and mosses, increasing the sense of magic.

wall or hedge – that leads to another part of the garden might be flanked by a pair of topiary balls, or the entrance to a kitchen garden be marked simply by a pair of wooden posts. These subtle markers indicate that you have arrived at a different place in the garden and their presence will increase your visual awareness of the space. The surface of the threshold itself can also be used to indicate a change of mood or pace, when it changes, say from grass to a pad of herringbone brick, so that as you walk through, your feet feel the difference in resistance and texture.

All these devices set up an element of intrigue and help to create the ceremonial of the journey. Tall, wide, wrought–iron gates flanked by urns or carved pineapples are an obvious statement about what is to be expected when you go through them. But you might want to prepare for an atmosphere of intimacy by making the entrance to a tiny courtyard very narrow, barely more than a gap in the hedge that you have to squeeze through. On the other hand, turning

ABOVE Many wrought-iron gates take inspiration from nature. Although this transparent gateway creates a boundary, it does not stop the viewer from peering through the unfurling metal leaves into the garden.

35

LEFT Large sun-bleached gates, with a simple capping of lead to protect the timber so that it will not need painting, provide a good balance with the sturdy rustic piers on either side.

RIGHT Time has stripped this door of its paint to reveal the original carpentry and finish.

FAR RIGHT A plain country picket gate marks the threshold of the garden, giving the visitor the sensation of stepping into a completely new environment.

the idea completely on its head, you could use a narrow opening to confound expectations, so that instead of bringing you into a confined area of the garden, it ushers you out into a wide-open space, perhaps a beautiful wild flower meadow.

The gates and doors themselves can create a particular impression instantly by their style or design. An old plank oak door that has been allowed to go silver-grey might pick up the essence of the house and give a sense of continuity. Timber doors and gates can be plain, painted, or finished with linseed oil. They can be made from reclaimed timber or

examples of skilled carpentry with intricate carving and mouldings. The door furniture is important and should be chosen carefully – a gate may open with a traditional thumb-latch or with a chunky cast-iron knob; hinges can be ornate or subtle. These details when well considered give a sense of place and suggest that there is something more to a garden.

Many gates are semi-transparent, allowing a view through. They might be made from metal bars, a panel of trellis or intricately carpentered chinoiserie work within the wooden frame. The desired effect might be achieved with narrow wooden laths or roundels or

pieces of reclaimed timber. Wrought-iron can be plain or heavily ornamented, and the metal doesn't always have to be painted; in some locations a rusty gate is perfect, if less practical.

Elswhere, the barrier between one area and another may be almost entirely transparent and, like an estate fence, be so uniform that you almost have to search along its length to find the gate. Or it may be the mechanism of a gate that engages you, as with a kissing gate, which imposes a dance-like progress through it. A similar way to make an intriguing arrival to a secluded space or secret garden would be to mimic the kissing gate with a staggered entrance of blocks of hedging that forces you to wind your way between them.

The function of every kind of entrance and opening is to slow the tempo and create pauses and resting places in the journey. By placing a metalwork arch with fragrant climbing roses over a gateway, you make a natural stopping place, and if this spot catches the late afternoon sun, it would be a natural place to put a small seat. These details do not need to be grand gestures, but they add to the experience of being in a particular garden.

LEVEL CHANGES

NORMALLY, THE BEST WAY TO DEAL WITH A SLOPING SITE is to terrace it by turning it into one or more levelled areas. Depending on the steepness of the slope, these will be held up by banks or retaining walls, or a combination of the two.

Creating level changes with grass banks is the most economical approach and offers by far the easiest method of creating a soft and natural difference between two levels. As a medium, grass banking is wonderfully flexible and can be used to combine and link the levels back into one another in an exceptionally fluid way. You might start in one part of the garden with, say, a 1.2m (4ft) high bank and end up in another with the bank a quarter of that height. If you have the space, the incline can be taken down gradually so that the bank becomes steadily shallower until it disappears into ground level.

In a contemporary setting, a sharply angled and moulded bank of mown grass that flows from one part of the garden to another creates a kind of architectural land art. At the other end of the scale, the grass on a bank can be grown long and planted with wild flowers and bulbs to soften it completely. To give the bank more vertical importance, emphasize the sculptural effect with wide platforms of hedging at the top of the bank. A good solution for an awkward change of level that interrupts the formality of a garden is to plant beech hedging into the slope. At the bottom of the slope the height of the hedge matches the height of the slope and gradually decreases following the line of the incline, so that slope and hedge become one. On a grander scale, sculpted grass terraces, like the beautiful example at Dartington Hall in Devon, offer inspiration for what

RIGHT This simple and very effective use of flint walls turns a sloping site into a beautiful banked amphitheatre. The series of level grass areas has a sculptural presence and creates a strong sense of place.

may be possible, but as a method of introducing a series of levels into a slope, terracing is usually associated with hard landscaping.

Dry-stone walls are among the most pleasing and non-invasive ways to create earth-retaining walls. In straight sections or following the contour of a slope, they can be built relatively easily up to a height of about 1m (3ft).

Good-looking retaining walls for a modern garden could be cast from concrete, then rendered and painted, forming smooth vertical surfaces. On gentler level changes, low brick-retaining walls can be built to

a variety of patterns, either straight or following the curve of a slope. These low walls double up as places to sit and could even have simple seats designed into them.

An ecological and economical method for dealing with small changes in level is to pile split logs one on top of the other to form a wall. Gradually plants will seed themselves between, and as the logs decay, will help to stabilize the bank.

When dealing with all but the most minor changes in level, it is best to consult a specialist. On very steep slopes, using a combination of retaining banks and walls will help to moderate the hardness of the walls.

ABOVE A formal garden on a sloping site will often have to be built on a series of level terraced areas. These level changes need to be accessed by steps.

RIGHT The lower, more formal lawn has been etched out of the original contours of the curved bank; the eating area is positioned at the true level of the bank.

STEPS

BELOW LEFT Dry-stone walling
has been used to form the risers
of these steps, tying in with the
dry-stone retaining walls on either
side. The steps link an intimate
eating terrace to the lawn above.

BELOW RIGHT Painting the risers
lime-green has given these simple
concrete steps an air of elegance
and modernity.

CHANGES IN LEVEL CALL FOR STEPS, AND THE CHOICE you have of materials, size and style is critical. The design of the steps and their 'importance' in the garden are likely to be influenced by where they are taking you and the particular mood you want to create.

If the setting is informal, materials that belong within the context are most suitable. Steps that wind up a gently sloping woodland walk can be made simply and easily from rustic poles and posts banged into the slope; in a relaxed area of the garden, they can be made from blocks of dry-stone walling.

In most cases, though, steps are made of hard landscaping, usually with brick and stone, either used separately or together. Since a flight of steps will have a strong visual impact on the landscape of the garden, the materials should be in keeping with the house walls or other areas of hard landscaping and, wherever possible, they should be local materials from local sources. Gradual slopes can accommodate long flights

of steps, but steep drops need shorter runs. In general, the steeper the gradient, the more complex will be the construction.

Steps need not follow a straight flight: half-landings offer an opportunity to pause and look back. A flight might have a half-landing and then continue straight upwards; at the half-landing, the steps might change direction or divide to become a double flight. Elegant sweeps and curves can be introduced with horseshoe- and crescent-shaped steps or concentric circles in the style of Lutyens. Details such as the design of a handrail, whether timber or iron, can also be used as a means to dress up or play down the importance of the staircase. Steps with an accompanying stone balustrade on either side have a very different weight, say, from a simple flight of steps and retaining wall with a single handrail.

There are standard specifications for the optimum depth and height of the treads and risers within a set of steps, and it is important that these are followed to

make ascending and descending safe and comfortable. These dimensions must be constant throughout the run of steps. The detailing and finish of the treads, though, can be treated in a variety of ways. Brick steps can be laid to a variety of patterns and, if the joints in the treads are left un-mortared and brushed with sand, this will allow plants to self-seed within them. Stone steps might have a bullnose or a flat-cut edge, and the treads be of riven or sawn stone, or be chisel-tooled with markings to make them less slippery when wet.

In a broad flight of steps, the sides might be left open and planted with thyme, or you could do the unexpected and have the planting in the centre with paving on either side. Alternatively, the surface of the treads might be limestone chippings with small plants sown in; in a set of steep steps and where safety considerations allow, a tiny hedge of clipped box or ivy planted in front of and to the same height as each riser, would give the impression of a living, green stairway.

LEFT These informal rustic
steps flow down the grass
bank like water from a spring,
blending beautifully into the
grassy setting.

The ancient art of topiary is traditionally applied to yew, as with these formal shapes, but other plants, such as hawthorn or, in hotter climates, olive, when clipped can appear just as magical, if not more so.

This allée of silver birch trees creates a striking and rhythmic pattern at all times of the year. The lightly dappled area at the feet of the soaring tree trunks has been planted with ferns and spring bulbs.

Tightly clipped domes of holm oak on clear stems create a mesmerizing allée in a formal garden.

The simple metal arches that form this tunnel create a long vista, transporting the traveller beneath its flowering canopy to a point further on in the garden.

An enchanting allée of closely planted lime trees with lichen-covered trunks at Cranborne Manor in Dorset.

TOPIARY, ALLÉES, TUNNELS, ORCHARDS

Despite their age, these old espaliered fruit trees are still able to produce fruit; their characterful structures are an added bonus.

Simple clipped cubes of box make a low division that allows movement between two distinct areas – ideal for a small garden.

TOPIARY

LEFT This ancient yew, which had in the past been clipped as topiary but then allowed to grow naturally, has gradually been brought back to form the main vertical sentinel in the centre of my own garden, re-creating the original garden axis.

CLIPPING DENSE FOLIAGE INTO CAREFULLY CONTROLLED, three-dimensional shapes has challenged and delighted gardeners through the ages. The shape of these 'plant sculptures' might be formal, fanciful or abstract. Topiary is a mark of a gardener's inventiveness, with the skill developing in an individual way in every gardener who practises it. An old specimen topiary will have passed through several generations of clipping hands and it becomes, in a very real sense, a biographical reference to all those people who have worked on it.

The art of topiary is ancient, with many surviving examples hundreds of years old. The bold shapes have long been used in gardens to introduce a sense of scale and drama. They can provide a strong vertical accent, and are often used to create focal points and as framing. A pair of clipped trees on either side of a gate or flanking an entrance, for example, perform a sentinel task, guiding you into the garden. In a less formal setting, you might have a single, large example of topiary to give height in a border, or growing out of the top of a hedge.

People usually think of topiary as being evergreen and, more often than not, yew (*Taxus baccata*), but there are alternatives. Box (*Buxus sempervirens*), beech (*Fagus sylvatica*), hornbeam (*Carpinus betulus*) or hawthorn (*Crataegus monogyna*) can be used to great effect. Different moods can be created according to the plant chosen. A double topiary walk planted entirely in yew would feel quite heavy, so to lighten it and break the rhythm, alternate yew and hawthorn could be used. The winter effect can be magical, especially with hawthorn, when the tightly knotted bare branches are unveiled after the tree has shed its

47

cloak of green, evoking a feeling of ancient hedgerows. Similarly, field maple (*Acer campestre*) can be clipped into a large dome, so that in winter the outline of the dome is filled in with the bare branches, on which there may even be lichens growing.

By way of complete contrast, a sophisticated design for a formal town garden might feature geometric topiary forms surrounded with limestone chippings around a minimalist pool of water. In this type of garden, where the most 'pared-down' planting is called for, the topiary takes the place of shrubs and trees, provides the essential height and creates strong lines and axes. Huge clipped cylinders make a bold contemporary statement, as would copper beech

(*Fagus sylvatica* 'Atropurpurea') clipped into 2m (6½ft) cubes, against a bright orange- or purple-painted wall.

Gardens with topiary are invariably full of character and atmosphere. The shapes can be geometric domes, cylinders or pyramids, or free-form abstract shapes that seem to have been sculpted by the wind. Topiary is also a great way to introduce some humour to a garden. Topiary peacocks are traditional, but other birds and animals lend themselves perfectly to the art. In a cottage garden setting, with chickens running around the fruit trees, you could have a group of topiary hens. And, in a semi-wild setting, such as an orchard or a flower meadow, unexpected geometric shapes would produce a surreal effect.

ALLÉES

LIKE AN AVENUE, AN ALLÉE IS A WALK BETWEEN
parallel rows of trees. The orderly, repeating pattern
of trunks, a planted colonnade, bestows a sense of
calm and quiet control. For the conceit to work, the
trees are usually of a single variety, often lime or
hornbeam, and must be of the same size and scale,
planted the same distance apart and of the same clear
stem height, so that they march together in equal
pairs. An allée is distinguished from an avenue by its
scale, with the trees planted quite closely together
and kept small by pruning and training, making it
specifically a garden feature.

Allées can be used to create beautiful cloistered
walks within the garden. They were a feature of many
Elizabethan gardens, used as meditative walks for the
ladies of the house, protecting them from exposure
to the sun, thereby preserving the fashionable paleness
of their complexions.

In addition to the more usual lime trees (*Tilia
cordata*) and hornbeam (*Carpinus betulus*), there are
a dozen different small-growing trees that might be
used in an allée, including quince, medlar, apple and
pear. A double row of hazels (*Corylus avellana*) might
lead into a wild or wooded part of the garden, and

RIGHT This closely planted
hornbeam allée has evolved from
a former double hedge and now
offers the ideal environment for
shade-loving spring flowers in
the dappled light at its feet.

stump crack willow (*Salix fragilis*), with its grey-green leaf, makes a lovely walkway for a country garden. In a garden with a warm climate, silver-grey olives (*Olea europaea*) or pungent citrus trees – oranges or lemons – would make a beautiful and atmospheric allée.

By definition, an allée will always comprise a pathway as well as trees, and the material used for the path, whether flagstones, brick, limestone chippings or just cut grass, will contribute to the overall feel that is created. The way in which the light falls on the path can be manipulated, either by pollarding the branches of the trees to allow the sun to filter through and create some dappled shade, or by allowing them to grow right over the top of the path, shutting out the light to create the magic of walking beneath a canopy of trees.

ABOVE This allée of holm oaks creates a very strong axis that gives scale to the garden and guides the traveller along its route towards a bench at the end, where one can sit and look back at the house.

TUNNELS

TREES, OR SOMETIMES CLIMBERS, TRAINED OVER A METAL structure to make an enclosed walkway, create a garden feature that brings structure, ornament and a strong sense of mystery to a garden. These tunnels may be clipped, formal and architectural, or soft, flowing and free-form; the type of plant will depend on climate as well as the degree of formality desired.

Pear and apple trees make particularly beautiful, as well as productive, tunnels, which are perfect along the route to a vegetable or kitchen garden. The tunnel could be composed of espaliers that, as well as growing vertically, bend round, forming a curve and joining in the middle. As time goes on and the trees become stronger and the branches thicker, the tunnel will become self-supporting, so the training structure can be removed or dismantled. At some later stage, you might decide to graft the branches of the individual trees together so that they hold 'hands' and become one organic unit.

Clipped hornbeam (*Carpinus betulus*) tunnels were frequently planted in seventeenth-century gardens, and they make beautiful architectural features, suitable for traditional as well as contemporary designs. Whitebeam (*Sorbus aria*) is another lovely subject for a tunnel and, in a warm climate, the Judas tree (*Cercis siliquastrum*), with its mass of purple-pink flowers, would be an arresting sight in early summer. A leafy tunnel of fig trees (*Ficus carica*) or grape vines (*Vitis vinifera*) leading to a vegetable plot or working area of the garden, would make the most lush and evocative walk in summer, dripping with clusters of grapes or filling the air with the rich scent of ripe figs.

Using climbing plants and allowing them to grow freely produces a softer, less formal effect. At the height of summer, a tunnel of fragrant roses and honeysuckle that has been planned to bring structure to a rambling garden, becomes an enticing and intoxicatingly perfumed walkway. Or, in a kitchen garden, a rusty metal tunnel could be used to support runner beans or other annual climbers such as sweet peas, nasturtiums and ornamental gourds.

Like pergolas, tunnels rely on a built frame to support the plants, but the experience of strolling within the formal, open-sided structure of a pergola is very different from the mysterious sensation of walking though the filtered green light of a planted tunnel. Here you are enclosed on all sides by branches and leaves; above you there may be flowers or fruit hanging down. For the duration of the 'journey', you are completely enclosed within the structure with all its textures and smells. In some gardens the element of complete enclosure can be a device for transporting you to a completely different part of the garden, and every time there is a little magic in the experience.

ABOVE The metal arches of this tunnel allow the fruit trees to be trained in a carefully thought-out and disciplined manner, making them as productive as possible. The tunnel also creates an axis that takes the visitor to the garden boundaries while framing the view beyond.

RIGHT When the desired height of these closely planted hazel trees was reached, the stems were bent over and pleached, or interlaced, to form a living, natural tunnel, as well as an enchanting intimate space.

ORCHARDS

ORCHARDS ARE MAGICAL PLACES. THEIR ESSENCE IS
fruitfulness and the continual rejuvenation of life.
Within them there is often an atmosphere of peace
and calm to be found, and a sense of security that
evokes the nostalgic world of childhood.

In an orchard, the ground beneath the trees is
naturally a little wild, and you can encourage this by
leaving the grass long, so that it becomes more like
a meadow. Alternatively, if the spacing between the
trunks is wide enough, you can cut the grass into
swathes of soft lawn, so that on hot days you can
throw down a rug and relax in the shade cast by the
trees. You could also create a gentle contrast within
the orchard itself by planting up the outer edges
with wild flowers, leaving the centre as a still green
glade of trees and grass.

RIGHT In warm climates, olive
groves carry the same appeal as
fruit orchards, enticing us to sit
in the shade under their branches
and enjoy the sense of peace that
they evoke.

LEFT Orchards provide a very simple way of achieving height within the garden. I never tire of their magic – from the tight pink buds in early spring, through to the autumn fruits and the gnarled and knotted pruned branches in winter.

In a different context, you might choose to create something that is more strongly patterned and formal, with the trees planted in regular rows, to form a strong grid with generous pathways between the rows. Alternatively, they might be laid out in the traditional quincunx (a triangular grid) pattern. To reinforce the geometry, you might plant a simple square of box hedging under each tree, or make an abstract pattern on the ground by planting small runs of hedging that wrap around and through the orchard like ribbons.

An orchard might comprise a single type of fruit tree, be a mix of apple, pear, cherry and plum, or it might be divided into two parts – one for 'pips', the other for 'stones'. Wherever trees are planted together in blocks of a similar height, a strong vertical accent is created. The blocks can be positioned so as to give weight within the overall layout of the garden. In my garden, the orchard acts as an anchor, counterbalancing the block of buildings on the other side of the garden and drawing you towards it.

Concentrating on pattern in the vertical dimension, you could reinterpret Russell Page's apple orchard, with its limewashed tree trunks, by limewashing the trunks of the fruit trees in coloured bands, perhaps pale blue or ochre, and using them to pick out a route through the orchard.

To thoroughly formalize an orchard, you might remove the traditional grass setting altogether. Imagine, instead, a symmetrical arrangement of perhaps a dozen small fruit trees emerging from a surface of limestone chippings. This would create an atmosphere that is both contemporary and unexpected, like a French courtyard with fruit.

horizontals

ABOVE A dark and tranquil
swimming pool sits neatly in a
daisy-studded lawn, while the line
of chestnuts planted along its
length add a sense of formality.

CENTRE This wild flower meadow
has a few luxurious old-fashioned
roses scattered among its grasses
and flowers, giving it the air of a
lost, romantic garden.

The horizontal plane in the garden comprises the surfaces that are used for gardening, circulating, relaxing and playing. This section deals with lawns, terraces, paths and their edging details; water in the form of ornamental and natural pools, and swimming pools; wild flower meadows and swathes of permanent planting, such as knot gardens, parterres and mazes. It also considers land sculpture, an art form that uses the techniques of earth sculpting and etching into the ground.

The horizontal plane is the given – the ground on which the garden is built. It is on this plane that the sense of scale and width in a garden is created, and it is the line that draws the eye on and links the garden with the surrounding landscape. A straight path may be used to reinforce this movement of the eye and emphasize a particular vista, or a path may be taken on a twisting, turning route to distract the eye from the far boundary.

The horizontal plane is tranquil, calming and reassuring, and it could be monotonous without pattern and surface variety. This section shows how the difference in surface textures and colours can be played upon to produce a range of effects. Grass may be long or short, and something as simple as the juxtaposition of these two contrasting textures can in itself be very powerful. Wild flower and prairie meadows are broad and level expanses, but they are given a sense of movement by the vertical

lines of the long grasses and the points of colour within them. The complex planted patterns made by knots, parterres, mazes and labyrinths add weight and form to a garden, and help to counterbalance the effect of strong verticals in the form of large trees or tall buildings.

The hard landscaping of terraces offers tremendous scope for variety, both in terms of texture and pattern. Brick paving makes a strongly patterned surface and can be an effective way of introducing textural interest to small areas. Smooth expanses of timber decking or sharply cut stone give a clean and crisp contemporary feel.

Land sculpture may sound impossibly ambitious for the average garden, but this section demonstrates that the simplest forms of earth sculpting can produce inspiring results. Where land sculpture has been introduced, the garden often has a deeply spiritual quality.

Water is surely one of the most exciting of the horizontal surfaces to play with in the garden environment. Whether clear and still or alive with movement from a fountain or cascade, it can be used as a vehicle to catch the sunlight and to reflect back images of surrounding trees or structures. In its moving form as a natural stream or rill, it brings life and vitality into a space and can act as a powerful line drawing the visitor towards its source or destination.

ABOVE A simple cut grass path under the canopy of old apple trees leads to a single seat at the far end of the walk. From here, one can look back and view the froth of flowers held in by neatly clipped box hedging.

This simple but effective herringbone pattern has been made out of peg tiles set on end. They can also be used to make panels that sit within a stone terrace to help break up otherwise over-large areas of stone and introduce another texture for contrast.

Cobblestones make a wonderful surface for a path or courtyard. If the joints are brushed with sand, mosses and self-seeding plants will colonize the gaps and soften the overall effect.

Randomly laid pieces of slate make a hard surface that can be used as an informal terraced area or to form pathways through the garden. Slate is also an ideal edging material when placed vertically in the soil to form a casual junction between a path and a border.

At the junction of a pebble path or in a small courtyard, interest can be added by changing the direction in which the pebbles are laid. This paving detail forms a simple, harmonious pattern that brings a focal point into the horizontal plane.

Textural interest has been created on the ground with alternate squares of chippings and grass. To develop the idea further, squares of stone and thyme could be used in a small courtyard or as small panels within a larger terrace.

Simple oak edging, which forms a raised bed and separates the herbs from the chipping path, has been enhanced by the addition of a cobalt-blue ceramic finial.

TERRACES, PATHS, EDGING

Roughly hewn stone provides a frame for pebbles that have been mortared down to form a hard and durable surface. In the gaps between the stone and pebblework, plants have been allowed to grow, creating a natural link.

Split timbers lined up neatly on an area of grass make a surface that can be walked on throughout the year. This type of pathway would suit a maritime or woodland environment perfectly.

When I am building brick terraces and pathways, I like to brush sand between the joints. This creates the perfect medium for mosses to grow, which will soften the surface and highlight the pattern of bricks.

TERRACES

BELOW A small flagstone
terrace surrounded by flowers
makes an intimate and scented
space that is conveniently
accessible from the house.

A VERSATILE AREA OF HARD LANDSCAPING ADJACENT
to the house is an essential part of a garden's design:
a place to spill out onto from the house, to put a table
and chairs – every garden should have somewhere for
sitting out at any time of year.

A terrace is also an arrival point. Even though it is
usually positioned on the private side of the house,
at the back or the side, it is still a place that you have
to cross before entering the house, and it acts as a
buffer zone between the house and the green part
of the garden. A terrace can be made out of a wide
variety of materials, from wonderful York stone
paving to herringbone brick, or a combination of
these and other materials.

The most important thing to establish when
designing a terrace is that the proportions are correct.
The length and width must be in balance with the
dimensions of the house. If it is not wide enough, you
will end up with something that looks more like a
path; a general rule of thumb for the width of a
terrace is one-third the height of the house.

The classic and most durable material for a terrace
is stone. It can be laid in a variety of ways, according
to the effect you wish to create. I particularly like to
allow plants to grow in the joints between the stones,
softening the hardness of the material. Terraces in
which hand-quarried flagstones of different sizes are
arranged to a random pattern around a keystone give

an air of informality and suit this kind of planted treatment. Heale House in Wiltshire has a superb example of just this kind of relaxed terrace, with its traditional English country-garden feel. In contrast, a terrace with large square blocks of machine-cut stone precisely laid gives a look that is crisp and contemporary. Another traditional method of laying stone that I like to use is parallel dressing: flagstones of the same width are laid in parallel rows, although each row may vary in width. This arrangement has a refinement about it that suits large terraces and formal situations. Whichever method you choose, avoid using too many small pieces of stone because they can end up looking like tiles.

RIGHT Making the most of sun and shade, this garden's wooden terrace beneath large and ancient trees and above a cool pool of water, leads to a sun-drenched stone terrace beyond.

ABOVE Keeping a balance between areas where you can sit and walk, and allowing the paving to become colonized by self-sown plants is an art in itself. But patient gardening, with time spent considering which plants to leave and which to take out, is well worth the effort.

LEFT Wooden decking makes a strong but soft horizontal surface that complements the crisp architectural lines of the timber-clad wall.

There are an infinite number of ways to add detail within the terrace itself. The outer band of stone might be hand-tooled with clawed or sparrow-peck marks, or be of a different colour stone. Stone or brick can be laid to form a frame around paving stones laid in a chequerboard pattern. An effective technique for gardens too small for a lawn is to mix limestones of different porosity to make the chequerboard. As the softer stones absorb moisture, they will acquire a patina of moss that contrasts with the clean, crisp surface of the hard stone. Or little pads of green can be introduced in a more controlled way, by planting tiny lawns of grass, thyme or camomile within the paving, or else a border of thyme that sits within the outer band of paving stones at the edge. A contemporary take on this would be to leave wide joints in between the slabs and plant them up with

mind-your-own-business (*Soleirolia soleirolii*). On a modern terrace of large, sharply cut stones, larger planting pockets incorporated into the paving can be filled with the rounded shapes of lavender or box balls, and used to guide you in a particular route across the terrace.

There are subtle ways of bringing water into the paving. A simply carved square indentation in a large slab forms a perfect square of water when it rains, or add a shallow rill that follows the edges of the paving. These details bring another level of interest to the area – including moving water in a very non-intrusive way would take it a step further. Your inspiration might be a particularly beautiful individual flagstone that has fossils in it or unusual veining. By installing a reservoir and pump underneath the flagstone and leaving narrow joints open around it, you can have a

RIGHT Making a paved area within a soft environment can be enough to add interest to what would otherwise be a rather plain and flat expanse of grass. This paving could form the central axis to the mown paths or be the base for a sculpture or an urn.

LEFT Paving or mosaic work can be very intricate, and panels like these should be used sparingly. They can make unique and exciting thresholds between one garden area and another – at a gate or doorway, for example, or even at the entrance to a house, where the skills of the artisan who designed and made them can be fully appreciated.

spring of water that bubbles up and washes gently over the stone, bringing out its markings and the richness of its colours. Whenever you want the stone to revert to an incognito part of the terrace, simply switch the pump off.

Brick is another versatile paving material, warm, tactile and a good pattern-maker. On its own, it is probably best for small areas, but it mixes well with other materials and is useful for breaking up large expanses of stone by adding texture and colour. Bricks can be laid flat or on edge, in herringbone, basketweave or other patterns, and the right brick for the situation depends, as always, on the context. Modern industrial brick gives the kind of crisp finish that suits a contemporary terrace; a small Tudor brick laid on edge in a herringbone pattern would add charm and detail to a small cottage garden. If the joints are left unmortared and simply brushed with sand, the brick will moss up beautifully – this is the method that I prefer to use for finishing brick paving. When selecting bricks, two things are vital: first, the

bricks' ability to withstand frost – too porous a brick will eventually crack and fracture; and second, the way the brick will weather and age. It is worth choosing a few samples and leaving them outside under a tree for six months or so, to see how they change.

Limestone chippings make a surface that is quick and easy to lay. Successive layers of good quality, hard crushed limestone (from 20mm to fines) are laid down, wetted and then compacted with a roller to make a smooth hard surface that looks crisp and formal.

In addition to these more traditional paving materials, there are plenty of other natural materials such as granite setts, cobbles and pebbles, that are readily available from garden centres and builders yards. They can be used in an infinite number of ways to personalize and add an element of artistry. A pebble mosaic might be made to commemorate a special event, a birth or the date the garden was built; it could be arranged in circles, squares or a sunburst, to make decorative panels within a larger stone or brick terrace. Sometimes in an old farmyard, you will come across areas of random paving composed of a mixture of materials, the bits of stone or brick that happened to be lying around at the time. Cotswold limestone in rough-hewn slices from the quarry can be laid on edge like herringbone. Square panels of peg tiles like those so often found in Lutyens and Jekyll gardens make an attractive detail within a terrace, or as an edge to a planting gap. Alternatively, a small area of granite setts laid out around an old wooden bench could be interplanted with creeping thymes or *Erigeron karvinskianus.*

A wooden surface lends itself to situations where a terrace connects with water, either around a swimming pool or in a seaside garden. The choice is extensive, from wide oak planks to narrow cedar boards that make a lovely scented surface after it has rained. As with stone surfaces, planting that spills over will soften the overall effect, and square planting pockets can be incorporated into the deck for trees, aromatic herbs like rosemary and sage, or big square beds of agapanthus.

ABOVE Covering the ground with limestone chippings has created a simple, inexpensive, yet elegant, terrace. The chippings combine a durable finish with a soft appearance.

PATHS

BELOW The texture of a path may have a particular function, such as slowing down visitors to the garden. These large round pebbles do this very well, causing people to linger by the lavender that spills over onto the path.

PATHS GIVE THE GARDEN AN ARCHITECTURAL BACKBONE by framing and linking the different parts and introducing a sense of proportion and scale, as well as providing a surface that is hard and dry. The width of a path is an important consideration, not only for practical reasons but also because it has a visual impact on the garden as a whole. A wide path will foreshorten the view, while a narrow path will give distance. You might also choose to play tricks with perspective; for instance, in a long thin garden you could make the path wide in relation to its length.

You also need to decide on the relative importance of the path and the kind of feeling that you want it to give. If it is a path leading to the front door, you will use it to greet visitors, so it should be wide enough for two people to walk along, side by side. If, however, the path is through a billowing cottage garden, have it only one person wide so that you brush past the plants as you travel along it, enjoying the scents and the colours of the flowers. The path might meander, too, slowing you down and prolonging the experience of being among the plants.

Once you have decided on the function of the path and the frequency of use, you can start to think about the texture and durability of its surface and how hard or soft it needs to be. This choice then indicates the path's function. A path that follows the main axis of the garden in herringbone brick or flagstones, for example, immediately has a certain grandeur, and tells you that it is a primary route.

In a garden of many paths there may be a hierarchy. The main route will be hard, durable and visible, while the smaller, tributary paths are likely to be softer, perhaps made of a material such as limestone

BELOW A narrow sinuous ribbon of brick runs alongside a mown grass path, defining the wild flower meadow that borders it and allowing a wheelbarrow to travel over its hard surface all year round. The path also draws the eye along its route into the distance.

chippings with plants growing within its surface. Here, walking becomes a different sensual experience as you move from a place that is hard, even and orderly into what is almost the plant kingdom. As you step on a crunchy surface, there is a change of pace and a sense of informality.

Paths create circulation through the garden and act as signposts, telling you there is a reason to go this way – a path may lead to a part of the garden where there is a fountain or a little arbour. In larger gardens, paths are also a means for switching the direction of the traveller, for offering choices: this way or that? At some point in the journey you could make the path widen out into a big square pad of paving with a bench positioned on one side. Sometimes you may want a path to be hidden, to go behind trees or

ABOVE Paths are important visual axes within the structure of the garden. This casually laid limestone path weaves through the flower borders to take the visitor through an opening in the hedge beyond and on into another area of the garden.

hedges that block the view. The path that disappears out of sight offers an enticement that is hard to ignore.

Paths can be read as a biography of the owner-gardener, reflecting the way they want you to travel through the garden. A passionate plantsperson will want you to experience the plants directly. Part of the journey through the garden may be along a path so narrow that the plants are hanging right over the edge. You might then have to move the plants gently aside and, in doing so, examine them in more detail. A path that is too wide is like a motorway, you rush along it without really noticing what is on either side.

Whatever the mood, formal or informal, a path must always be functional. If it is the main delivery route to the front door, a narrow winding path will

LEFT When there is sufficient width, as in the case of this beautifully laid flagstone path, plants can be allowed to grow in the joints between the stones. Here, they can be appreciated close-up, and also help soften the otherwise hard lines of the paving.

ABOVE Paths need not always be straight or flat. This path has a wonderful bold curve, hugging the plants at its edge as it winds through the garden. It also has a very slight camber, making it feel both natural and informal.

FAR LEFT Laid upside down, these bricks make an interesting textured pattern. The indents of the bricks become pockets for grass and mosses, and the curve adds interest, drawing the traveller on through the wooded part of the garden.

certainly not be appreciated by anyone, but a path that gets less use, say, one leading to a herb garden, could be made of cobbles with a little pebble mosaic set into the middle, so that you can't help but slow down and smell the herbs.

As with terraces, you can use the paving materials for a path in a variety of ways. A stone path might have mortared joints or just be made of plain stones butted up together; it could have bands of brick running up the sides to accentuate the length. If it is very long, it might have squares of brick or low-growing thymes within it to break up the length and slow the eye down. This would be a good way to deal with a path running along one side of a long narrow town garden. It is also important to consider

how different materials react to the elements. A York stone path that runs along the shady side of the house could be dangerously slippery when damp, whereas the textured surface of a brick path will give a much better grip.

Paths don't always need to be made of a hard material, and there are many ways to make simple but functional pathways for very little outlay. A mown path makes a lovely route through longer grass, perhaps leading to a gate or an orchard. Paths made of cinders or ash are traditional for kitchen or vegetable gardens. Sometimes stepping stones set into grass are right for the situation, and where a path is needed over damp ground or a marshy area, a stilted decking walkway is a good solution.

EDGING

EDGING ADDS INTEREST AND INTRICACY AT CLOSE
quarters in the garden. Like a line drawn in ink, it gives
distinction to the surfaces that it borders and separates.

The function of the edging is likely to influence
the materials you select for it. A band of stone, say,
50cm (20in) wide along a herbaceous border helps
with maintenance and the upkeep of the lawn, and
also allows you to plant right up to the border's edge.
The plants can tumble out onto the flagstones and, at
the same time, the stone gives a frame to the border
and defines it. A path of limestone chippings that has
been planted with spreading thymes might be given a
brick band on either side to formalize it and to retain
the soft surface with a definite edge.

A herbaceous border needs a generous edge, so
that the plants can be allowed to grow naturally; on
the other hand, an edge running between a lawn and
a path may need to be no more than a single discreet
brick placed on its edge.

Traditional Victorian edging tiles are perfect in
a kitchen garden; I like to use them with brick,
laying the brick frog face down, then putting the tile
behind. This gives you a gap for cutting the grass
right up to the edge of the bed while the tile holds
back the soil. A variation on this is to replace the
edging tiles with bricks standing on end or vertically
at a 45-degree angle.

Giving a lawn an invisible edge of mild steel is
a particularly good way to maintain the purity of the
green swathe. The metal edge finishes flush with
the lawn, keeping the edge trimming to a minimum
and preserving the lines and formality. Steel can also
be pre-formed and bent into all sorts of interesting
shapes, including circles and curves. With their small

unit size, brick and granite setts work well as edges
for shallow arcs, but on tight curves the joints
become too wide and the effect can be ungainly.

Softwood timber edging is a more affordable
option, but should be used where it is not too visible,
say, along the edge of a newly planted hedge. The
wood will eventually rot, but by this time the hedge
line will be well established. For a more formal edging
in important parts of the garden, use a hardwood,
such as oak or elm. A detail that I like to use to create
slightly raised beds is an edge of weathered oak,
which is softer in feel than stone or brick.

BELOW In my own garden,
metal edging has been used to
keep the formal lines of the lawn
crisp and pure. It has been left
unpainted, so that the steel takes
on a surface covering of rust,
giving it the appearance of soil.

As well as manufactured edges, there are numerous edgings that can be created from natural materials that might be lying around the garden. Small boulders, large pebbles and naturally hewn stone such as slate can all be used with varying degrees of formality to define edges, from a band of pebbles along a path to a few well-chosen stones strategically placed to guide you along a trodden-earth path. Living edges of box, rosemary or chives are decorative in kitchen gardens, as are country edges like hazel hurdles, small metal hoops, driftwood, or coppicing made into a criss-cross trellis and tied with sisal.

LEFT Natural stone has been laid on edge to form a band separating the lawn from the house. In this context, it doubles as a drainage channel, but could equally well be translated as a beautiful edge to a border.

BELOW This organically woven hazel edge is the perfect device for keeping herbs and vegetables within the bounds of their borders.

The earth has been formed into flowing shapes, adding a textural quality to the land form. The close-clipped grass surface of the mounds is emphasized and thrown into relief by the tongues of shade on either side.

There is something magical about long grasses – the way in which they change colour, moving through shades of green to a pale straw as the seasons pass, and the drama they create when the early morning or evening sun shines through their seed heads.

This naturalistic meadow-style of planting is given weight and punctuation by the addition of lilies and other flowering plants. The bridge connects to an even wilder environment.

Lawns need not be of grass. In a contemporary city garden, a large square or rectangle planted with barley or a single variety of long grass, creating a sheath of green all at one level, can be an extremely stimulating alternative.

Slim grass strips set at regular intervals within chippings could be the starting point for a new and exciting semi-green surface for incorporating into a small garden or courtyard.

LAWNS, LAND SCULPTURE, MEADOWS AND PRAIRIE PLANTING

These bold grass banks incorporate flights of shallow, sculpted grassy steps, which flow naturally and easily between the different levels.

RIGHT This beautifully tended
lawn sweeps gracefully up and
into a long grass barrow, creating
a mysterious and compelling
feature – a hidden area of garden.

FAR RIGHT A simple steel edge
gives this lawn definition and
formality, as well as raising it
above the level of the path.

LAWNS

MENTION LAWNS AND, FOR MOST PEOPLE, THE IMAGE that springs immediately to mind is the traditional English, striped greensward. But there can be so much more to a lawn than an area of plain mown grass, creating different effects with cutting heights or using different plants within the grass.

Take inspiration from nature or from art, and you can create effects that are beautiful and striking. A lawn could drop down in a series of concentric squares, each square lower by a couple of centimetres, with the edges held in place by a metal strip, so that the effect is like embossed paper. Or, using the same method, take an abstract painting and literally translate it into a contemporary lawn, in which the squares and circles are just grass at different levels and each of the sunken areas shows up as a subtle difference in shadow. By cutting the grass at different heights, as I have done at home, you can create a grass parterre that costs absolutely nothing at all. Just lay out a pattern with markers and string and then cut short paths through it. It could be a series of squares formed of long grass and short grass, or a pattern of wavy lines like ribbons.

A large lawn can be transformed by creating a pattern of four large rectangles of long grass planted with a mass of daisies, with close-cut paths in between. The best way to differentiate the areas is to cut the rectangles with a rotary mower and the paths with a cylinder mower, then use lawn weed-killer on the grass paths to underline the contrast and pick out the perfect rectangles of longer grass and daisies. And lawns need not be completely weed-free. Daisies, ajuga, even creeping buttercup, can turn an area of grass into an area like textured embroidery.

Levelled, sunken lawns, like Edwardian tennis courts, can be used for tennis, croquet or bowls, with the sides formed into gentle grass slopes where you can sit and watch. And does a lawn even have to be level? Why shouldn't it be like waves, a series of little hummocks that ripple across the garden, so that in the evening as the sun sets there will be shadows coming over the grass? This very gentle form of land-sculpting is a beautiful way of introducing movement into the garden. If there are hills in the background, why not bring them into the garden and echo the shapes with miniature hills and dips in the grass? Or, have a lawn that sweeps up into a little rounded hummock no more than 50cm (20in) high, where you can sit, just above the level of the garden. For a change, make a crazy, temporary spiral of daisies in the grass, by using a lawn weed-killer but leaving the spiral untouched.

A lawn does not even have to be grass. You could use white clover, as I have done for a garden in France, where it was too hot and dry for the lawn to stay green. A high proportion of white clover was put in with the grass, and the whole lawn became a magnificent, contemporary horizontal of white flowers. Lawns can have primroses in them; they can be like flowery meads in spring, coming alive with bulbs and flowers and kept short for the remainder of the year.

In really large areas of mown grass, you might choose to alter the height of the cut in just one part – the centre or one corner. This then becomes the more intimate space within a large expanse, a place where you feel at home. You can alter the perspective and bend the sense of scale to make an area that feels special, simply by maintaining this one area to a higher standard than the rest.

There are inspirational lawns like artist Chris Parson's Dew Garden at Aylesbury in which he brushes patterns into the early morning dew. The effect is transient but magical, lasting a few hours, then fading away. Other horizontal green areas could be made of thyme or camomile, though these are only really practicable on a small scale and in sun. To make a pool of green in a shady area where grass won't grow, you might increase the dampness of the spot and cultivate a moss garden.

Natural grass areas of all kinds offer inspiration for new ways to make lawns. You can tell an ancient meadow by the hummocks: these are the ant hills that have become grassed over the years. Bumpy, tussocky surfaces or the ancient traces of ridge and furrow patterns can also be given a new twist by making slick

FAR LEFT Within my own courtyard garden, which is sheltered and warm early in the year, I have planted large drifts of snowdrops, aconites and *Crocus tommasinianus*, creating a carpet of spring flowers. This is a marvellous way of giving a sense of maturity to a new garden.

BELOW This truly beautiful contemporary lawn of thymes has been created by Dan Pearson. These ground-hugging aromatics entice you to walk carefully along the very narrow path towards the planting of ox-eye daisies, releasing their fragrance as you tread gently on their leaves.

versions that fit into a contemporary setting. Or maybe you have a lawn that is naturally uneven, so why alter the lie of the land to make it flat? Why not instead choose to cultivate and enjoy it? Large areas of plain lawn can be daunting. Creating areas within them that have a distinction, however slight, provides intimacy. A wide band of wild flowers around a lawn frames and humanizes the space. In July, mow it back to the same length as the rest of the grass or, instead, plant the frame with autumn crocus or colchicums, so that in September a faint, pale lilac haze hovers over the edges of the lawn.

Allowing areas of the grass to mature and go through their seasonal cycle is another way to introduce pattern. You could keep cut paths or patches of short grass among the long grass; the short grass is kept mown, while the rest is allowed to grow and set seed, and cut back once the cycle is complete. If you want to make a gentler change, you might mow it to

leave a broad U-shape of longer grass just where a bench is placed, so that the seat nestles into it.

Inspired by the traditional striped lawn, there are some beautiful examples of patterned garden floors that are part-lawn, part-hard surface such as brick or limestone chippings, laid in strips to form a rhythmic pattern across the ground. This kind of contemporary surface does need careful maintenance to keep it looking good, but would work well in a small space or town garden.

Finally, why do we insist on raking away leaves the instant they fall on the lawn, or gathering all the fallen apples when some might be left for the birds to eat? Obviously a certain amount of tidying is part of essential lawn maintenance, but there is a beauty about fallen leaves and windfall apples. A lawn can and should be a magical green space that is at one with the seasons, rather than a flat and sterile expanse of uninteresting grass.

LAND SCULPTURE

LAND SCULPTURE INVOLVES MOULDING THE ground into patterns that are then grassed over; these patterns could be mounds, grass walls or turf labyrinths. Also known as land art, land sculpture can be used to add a subtle extra dimension to the garden without dominating it; at its simplest level, it means digging into the ground and making earth mounds with the soil you have taken out. Larger-scale earth sculpting involves removing the topsoil from the area that is going to be moulded and digging out the subsoil before replacing the topsoil and re-seeding it with grass. Although this needs to be done with a mechanical digger, it is not a hugely expensive operation.

Sculpting the earth is a beautiful and lyrical way of alleviating the dullness of flat expanses or of reintroducing some natural form into a garden that has become sterile through lack of interest. It brings a quality of serenity and spirituality.

A good technique for introducing character into a featureless piece of flat ground is to cut a shallowly banked amphitheatre into it and then allow the grass to grow back on top of the banks. You could either cut the grass close or leave it to grow long. Alternatively, if you have, say, a huge flat expanse of grass and you want to introduce a very subtle change, you could make the ground roll in a series of 3m (10ft) bands that will give a sense of movement and catch light, dew and frost. From a distance, the area will be viewed simply as grass, but as you approach the pattern will emerge.

Another really simple method of land sculpting within a lawn area, whether large or small, is to etch a path into the ground. This involves taking out

ABOVE This grass mound sits in my own garden. I love to walk around the spiral to the top and look over the rest of the garden and across to the surrounding countryside. The elevation also allows another perspective of patterns in the garden.

FAR LEFT An earthwork consisting of a series of grassed earth banks; although not very precisely made, they have all the charm of a Bronze Age settlement. The earth has been dug out and piled up into concentric rings, rising up at one side to the intriguing little garden building with its turf roof. At the centre of the earthwork stands a rough-hewn piece of timber.

about 30cm (1ft) of earth and then grassing it over. The effect is one of an ancient track that has been gradually trodden down over the years and, when viewed from the distance, it will show as a subtle ribbon pattern in the grass. In a more contained space, you might choose to etch a spiral pattern into the lawn that will, in turn, become the perfect location for a seat.

Land sculpting can also be viewed as a form of ground topiary, and grass is certainly not the only form of groundcover that can be used for this. You might take inspiration from the natural growth habit of mound-forming herbs or dense-leaved plants like box or billowing rosemary, and plant them into the contours, so that they become an organic part of the shaping. Even on a very small scale, low hummocks of thyme planted in the centre of a stone terrace could make an intriguing landscape in miniature, forming a ruggedly humpy rug, or a series of small ripples.

MEADOWS AND PRAIRIE PLANTING

WE TEND TO ASSOCIATE MEADOW AND PRAIRIE PLANTING with huge gardens that have acres of land attached. But this kind of planting really doesn't have to be in a field or a paddock. It is quite possible to create an enchanted wild space within the confines of any garden, even a small town garden.

A meadow project might begin with a decision to have less or no mown grass in one part or all of the garden, and to have in its place a grass area that is natural and more bio-diverse. Drawing inspiration from natural planting associations, you could select grasses such as quaking grass (*Briza maxima*) and deschampsias, then introduce the flowers, maybe sanguisorbas with wild blue geranium and achilleas, or ox-eye daisies and clover. For a spring-flowering meadow, you could choose primroses, cowslips and fritillaries. It is also possible to introduce herbaceous perennials into the meadow environment as well: phlox, wild scabious, chicory, even onopordum – the huge silver thistle. This kind of planting holds hands with the cultivated part of the garden, and the results can be very exciting. Imagine a swathe of long grass with perhaps red clover flowering and then the silver leaves and majestic flowers of onopordums emerging from the soft haze. The effect is a terrific positive-negative – a hefty thistle in an ephemeral setting.

Even if your preference is for the look and feel of an authentic wild flower meadow, you can still include a few of the taller cultivated perennials, like monkshood or cephalaria. You will see bold plants like eupatorium growing in meadows; in the Lake District, you will come across wonderful *Cirsium hederifolium* growing 1.5m (5ft) high in the grass

verges. So why not grow its relative *Cirsium rivulare* in your meadow, and have its intense magenta flowers coming out of the grass? Alternatively, you could choose the vivid lipstick-pink form and have it with acid-green grasses, following on from pale blue camassias that flower early in the season.

Grass is the natural habitat of many familiar herbaceous plants. Take a plant like pulsatilla, for instance, which is usually seen planted in rockeries or herbaceous beds, and not in its natural environment. By putting it back into a meadow setting, you are, in a sense, liberating it.

ABOVE This prairie meadow style of planting is a striking interpretation of the native North American meadow. The trick when creating such new and naturalistic plantings in the garden is to use a limited palette of grasses and flowering plants.

ABOVE These stately white onopordums, with their ghost-like structure, create large-scale drama within this meadow, and they become even more ethereal when viewed during a full moon.

A meadow, like a lawn, need not be level, so why not scoop part of it out, make it more moisture-retentive and create a tiny microclimate that has trollius, forget-me-nots and other damp-loving plants growing within it? Sometimes, accidental plantings can provide the inspiration for unusual plantings that might not otherwise have been considered. You often see garden plants that have escaped into the wild or survived in a neglected garden that's gone back to grass. In my own orchard, the grass is full of spring bulbs, and suddenly last year some beautiful pale mauve flowers

standing about 1m (3ft) high also appeared. They turned out to be the flowers of some scorzonera, the vegetable oyster, which I'd allowed to go to seed in my vegetable garden.

Then there are all the annual meadow flower mixes of corn cockle and poppies, which are resown each year. A wonderful, loose planting could be composed of black opium poppies, cornflowers, clary sage and nigella. Many of the seed companies that sell wild flower mixes also offer wild grass mixes; they can separate out the individual species for you, so you could have a meadow, say, of quaking grass with no flowers at all.

There are many different ways of bringing this natural style of planting into the garden, even growing wild flowers formally between box hedges or in a wide band around the lawn. Garden meadows do not have to be exact or authentic and there is nothing to prevent you from making an artificial meadow that takes the feel and atmosphere of the real thing, but uses plants that suit the conditions of the particular garden. We have been conditioned into thinking that a meadow can only be outside the garden, or that a meadow looks pretty for a while and then the grasses collapse. But not all grasses collapse; deschampsias, for instance, stay upright and carry on looking good throughout the season. It is just a question of observing how plants grow and perform in the wild, looking at the type of soil they grow in and the plants they associate with, and then using this knowledge to bring them into the garden.

There are still other ways to take inspiration from what's outside the garden boundaries. You could move away from meadow grasses altogether and use

an annual crop such as barley. Sown in four large blocks into the lawn area and with black cornflowers planted in, the result is dramatic and different. In a large new garden, this planting could be made while you are waiting to develop the garden, and it will cost you virtually nothing.

Another option to consider is a large square bed edged with box hedging that you cultivate each year. Sow it with pale blue flax and white corn cockles combination for an absolutely stunning look. It also gives a contemporary feel because, by introducing a commercial crop into a garden setting, you have done something unexpected. Planting in this way makes a strong visual impact. How marvellous if, in a town garden, you do the very opposite of what's expected and, instead of a lawn, have a cornfield with a path that runs through the middle to an area right in the centre where you can sit, surrounded by corn.

Prairie planting is very closely linked to meadow planting in terms of its use of space within a design, but it has a much richer species-base of plants and a greater proportion of flowers to grasses. Some of the best prairie meadows are those in America, planted with enormous swathes of echinacea and rudbeckia. Prairie meadows tend to grow in places that bake in summer and where the grasses don't do that well, but the main impact comes from the perennial flowers. A prairie meadow in the English climate would be different; it would be greener and more like the meadows talked about earlier, with tall herbaceous plants growing among the grasses.

Wherever you are adapting a particular style of planting to suit different conditions, the most important thing is to observe and learn from the natural habitats, look at how the plants are growing together and keep to combinations that feel right.

LEFT Spring-flowering bulbs
are one of my favourite ways
of introducing an extra layer of
interest to meadow plantings.
Here, casually planted tulips make
an unexpected appearance in a
natural grass area, which, in turn,
gives the planting a modern feel.

FAR LEFT Within these squares a
variety of wild flowers are allowed
to grow, and the grid-like layout
of the meadow is criss-crossed by
a series of mown paths that link
the whole area together.

When creating a knot garden or parterre, I prefer to use a single plant species but vary its form by careful pruning and clipping. Here, square-clipped box hedges make an effective contrast with the central ball.

This intricate geometric pattern of interlocking squares has been given extra definition and texture by using two different varieties of box, creating a subtle colour change.

Knots and parterres are best viewed from above. They might become more visible as one travels up a flight of steps to another garden level, or when seen from an upper floor room, where the pattern – simple or complex – can be revealed.

Box hedging has been clipped with a rounded top to complement the pattern of the spiral, giving this parterre a very fluid form. This technique can be used on a large or a small scale.

A copper beech maze, seen here before the hedges have been cut, has a softness that hides its puzzle well. Once clipped, the geometric pattern will be unveiled, changing the atmosphere completely.

KNOTS AND PARTERRES, MAZES AND LABYRINTHS

Hedges can be cut at different heights within a knot, as in this pattern where the plants weave in and out of one another to form continuous undulating ribbons of green.

These simple geometric shapes with their subdivisions can be used either for planting or left empty to emphasize the pattern still further.

KNOTS AND PARTERRES

KNOTS AND PARTERRES HAVE YEAR-ROUND INTEREST.
They introduce horizontal swathes of texture into the
garden that look their most breathtaking in winter,
crisply outlined in frost or softly cloaked in snow.

The art of making patterns in the ground with
clipped plants is an old one, and although box is the
material traditionally associated with these ornate
patterns, there is no need to be limited to a single
plant when making knots and parterres. If a plant can
be clipped, then it can be used, and the pattern can be
as tiny or as large as you like.

Knots are usually conceived as small, intimate
spaces, somewhere between 1.2 and 3.6m² (4 and
12ft²), with the height of the hedging no more than
45cm (18in). Parterres are usually grander in scale and
concept. The patterns were originally designed to be
viewed from above, from the main living quarters on
the *piano nobile*, where the gardens could be seen,
spread out on the ground like precious brocades.

French and Italian Renaissance parterres were often
laid out in very elaborate patterns of box as potent
indicators of the wealth and status of the house-
owners, who were able to employ an army of
gardeners to maintain miles of immaculately clipped
hedges. What remains of the parterres at Hampton
Court is only a fraction of what once was there.

Knots and parterres make good anchor points, and
can be used in parts of the garden where extra weight
is needed. The playfulness of the patterns may invite
you to wander through them; sometimes the knots are
planted up, sometimes left empty. The ground may be
grass or limestone chippings, a sand or shell mix, or
little brick paths. The planting can be box on its own
or box mixed with santolina or another small-leaved
plant like berberis. Mixing the plant materials allows
you to create tapestries of different textures and
colours; or the same plant in different colours, say,
green and gold box, might be interwoven to form a

BELOW Knots and parterres can
be used as frames for a wide
range of planting styles. Here,
a bold and simple drift planting
of lychnis contrasts superbly with
the emerald-green of the box.

LEFT This parterre with its round-
topped hedges brings a green and
calming influence to the heat of a
sun-drenched garden, and entices
all who enter to walk, wander and
discover its many routes.

ABOVE Parterres do not have to
be made of hedges. In my garden,
grass mown at different heights
creates a lawn parterre, which
comes to life especially when the
low sun shines across it and
enhances the pattern.

beautiful lover's knot. Rosemary and lavender, like
santolina, make beautifully aromatic hedges, as does
fragrant myrtle (*Myrtus communis*), provided the
climate is warm enough, but the essential feature of
the knot is that the hedges are kept clipped, not left
to grow naturally.

The character and setting of a garden usually
suggest a style for the knot or parterre, and the
pattern may be complex and ornate or simple, such
as repeated cubes of hedging, with small gaps between
them. The number of variations that can be played
on a single simple design is illustrated by the example
of a pattern composed of interlocking cubes and

L-shaped brackets. Both the cubes and the brackets
could be in box, or the cubes could be box and the
brackets beech (*Fagus sylvatica*). If the design is planted
all in box, it will have a calmness about it that remains
consistent throughout the year. If the box is mixed
with beech, the element of change is introduced: in
spring and summer there will be the slight difference
in leaf shape and colour, which in winter becomes
more dramatic as the beech turns to russet and a new
pattern emerges. To make a pattern of stronger colour
contrasts, the box might be mixed with copper beech
(*F. sylvatica* 'Purpurea') instead of green, giving
repeated blocks of purple and green. Or the whole

design could be planted in green beech, so that the summer calm turns to russet in winter and creates an altogether different seasonal mood. Topiary trees planted within the parterres would add another layer of textural interest and contrast.

Using unexpected materials within the conventional patterns, such as a summer infill of green barley in open squares edged with box, creates something that looks contemporary. Equally, a modern parterre can be made to look old: if the parterre is planted in grass but with gaps left here and there in the pattern, it will appear as though some of the hedges disappeared years ago.

Once the overall scale, pattern and materials of the parterre are decided, other factors need to be considered. Will the style be formal or informal? Could it be planted in a very contemporary garden overlooking a natural landscape? Could you have it in a part of the garden that you use mostly in summer, where there is a swimming pool, and an equal weight of planting is needed to counterbalance the horizontal block of water? In this situation, you might take an area the same size as the pool, and plant the parterre with a tall, transparent plant like *Verbena bonariensis* that would sit within the box and allow the pattern to be read through a veil of flowers all summer. In winter, the box pattern would dominate again, distracting the eye away from the hibernating pool.

If a knot or parterre is defined principally as the laying down of a pattern so that it can be read from above, it follows that the material need not necessarily be a hedging plant. It could be something more temporary, something as simple as a pattern of grass squares that comes and goes. At home, I have just

created a wild flower parterre made up of formal shapes of long wild flower grass and mown paths. Or, you could mix a lawn parterre with hedging, so that you have, for instance, three big diamond shapes of wild flower grass and cut grass going into three clipped box diamonds, going back into grass, and so on.

It all comes down to the kind of mood and atmosphere that you want to create with this pattern, and the degree of permanence. An ephemeral parterre that completes its life cycle in a year has a beauty of its own. The simplest parterre of all might be squares filled with flax, created in a single season and costing virtually nothing.

ABOVE This amusing parterres, with its clipped hummocks, becomes a textural sensation that one wants to explore, touch and be a part of.

MAZES AND LABYRINTHS

LEFT A large maze of clipped yew at Hatfield House in Hertfordshire creates a striking contrast to the vertical lines of the trees in the background. This juxtaposition underlines and emphasizes the strong geometry of the maze.

MAZES AND LABYRINTHS ARE PATTERNED ELEMENTS LIKE knots and parterres, but taken a step further to give a sense of journey to the pattern. They can range in size and scale from elaborate rooms of clipped hedging to the smallest spiral of pebbles arranged on a flat surface.

Sometimes square, sometimes circular, many of the patterns are ancient and appear in myth and legend as journeys to be negotiated. More recently, they have been planted to amuse and entertain, with hedges high enough for people to lose themselves on their journey. To make a distinction between the two, I think of a maze as a game, with a beginning and an end, and a labyrinth as being a series of hedge patterns that muddle and mislead.

A contemporary maze on a large scale could be composed of a mixture of different materials, starting on the outside with a hedge, then moving onto a turf wall, then back to hedge, then onto a dry-stone wall. As you travel through the maze, going in, coming out again, taking the wrong path, you would find yourself endlessly going past hedging, turf wall, hedging, dry-stone wall. Then, perhaps when you reach the middle, you find there something precious, maybe a piece of beautifully cut or carved stone that tells you that you have finally arrived.

Mazes and labyrinths can be made of mown paths or cut into the ground. There is no need for them to be large. A maze pattern on a terrace might be made by just lowering the level of the stone slightly so that it holds water when it rains, or it could be planted with creeping thymes or laid out in a soft, porous stone so that, as time passes and the stone absorbs moisture, it becomes covered in moss and writes the pattern out in green.

BELOW A turf labyrinth etched into the ground creates a wonderful brocaded pattern in an otherwise plain lawn, adding an essential dimension of fun and play within the garden.

Mazes in orchards seem to have a particular air of magic about them. In the orchard of a Norfolk garden, I have made two copper beech mazes – one square, the other circular. One leads you straight into the centre, and then you have to search to find your way out; the other reverses the puzzle, so that you actually have to search to find the way in. Hedge mazes need to be high enough to prevent you from seeing over the top or being able to read the whole pattern immediately from the outside. But don't be put off the idea; a maze need not be on a grand scale to be

effective: you could plant a labyrinth of parallel hedges no more than 3m² (10ft²) and use it as a semi-division across a long narrow garden. To get to the far end of the garden, you have to weave your way though the pattern so it slows your journey and at the same time creates a kind of dance with the materials, like an interactive knot garden. In addition, the pattern can be read from above, looking down from the house.

In traditional mazes, such as the fine example at Hatfield House in Hertfordshire, there would often have been a mound in the centre, so that on reaching

your goal, you could look out and be seen, as well as enjoying the bafflement of those still trying to reach the centre. There is something wonderful about these interactive elements in gardens large enough to house them, involving children and whole families. They introduce humour and playfulness, and prevent gardens from becoming overly serious and static.

At Glendurgan in Cornwall, an old maze of cherry laurel (*Prunus laurocerasus*) is planted into the steep natural slope of the valley. From the opposite slope, the pattern is clearly visible, but from the maze side

itself there is no way of reading the pattern. An alternative version for a maze on a slope might be to make the height of the hedging work against the lie of the land, so that at the bottom of the slope the hedge is at its highest, and at the top at its lowest, so from time to time you get glimpses out.

Mazes should have some reward at their centre. You might make a hedge maze that has another small maze in the middle, this one made of pebbles, perhaps, so that at the heart of the maze another mystery remains to be unravelled.

BELOW This turf maze draws visitors into its pattern, making them take decisions at every turn. When they eventually find the way to its centre and climb the ladder, they can look back on the twists and turns of their contorted route.

A straight and formal line of water, softened with native planting at its edges and at the surface, creates a strong visual axis towards and away from the bench.

Water is as magical in small quantities as it is in large. This simple rill can be an inspiration for many other water features in the smaller garden.

Mossy stones snake their way through calm, shallow water, adding a pattern to the reflective surface, as well as daring us to walk across.

This contemporary pool is connected beautifully to an upper level by the water that pours through a chute, enticing us to explore its source.

This classic swimming pool, designed by Thomas Church, achieves a balance between the man-made and the natural. Its fluid lines and the clear water are emphasized by the placing of a rock at the water's edge.

ARCHITECTURAL WATER, NATURAL WATER, SWIMMING POOLS

The deep blue water of this swimming pool creates a mirror in which the stonework is reflected, allowing a strongly repeated contrast between verticals and horizontals.

This stream forms a wonderful division within the garden. The simple and elegant timber walkway spanning its width connects two parts of the garden, allowing the visitor to cross and recross an otherwise impassable boundary.

RIGHT In a natural woodland setting, a spring has been channelled into a straight and narrow rill. Its stone edges soak up the moisture and have become encrusted with moss.

ARCHITECTURAL WATER

THE HISTORICAL PREDECESSOR OF THE RILL IS THE irrigation channel and, although the purpose of the rill now is largely ornamental, it retains something of its essential integrity as the lifeline of a garden. At Rousham House in Oxfordshire, a delightful stone rill weaves a sinuous path through the garden, catching the light and guiding the traveller to the point at which it meets an octagonal pool.

These artful, man-made water channels harness our natural attraction to water, and add an essential element of mystery – the need to know where it leads and to follow it back to its source or on to its end point. They perform the service of magic in the garden, drawing the eye as they run through the garden like a silver thread.

A rill should be narrow, generally not more than 20–30cm (8–12in) wide overall. It may be contained by stone, brick or pebble, and it may be moving or still, straight or winding. The choice of material will depend on the style and character of the garden. A contemporary rill could be made of a hard stone like granite, which will maintain the crisp, clean lines of the edges, whereas softer limestone will gather moss, becoming less visible in time and merging with the grass or planting around it.

LEFT In this garden, there is the choice of walking along the edge of the water or crossing it. The wooden decking seems to float on the water's surface, enforcing the natural qualities of the material.

BELOW A long narrow rill leads the eye into the distance and, at the same time, draws the visitor towards its edge, where the falling water introduces an element of intrigue and magic.

Unless the run is a short one, rills carved out of stone tend to be costly, and a less expensive method is to cast the channel in poured concrete, give it a waterproof render and then line the sides with brick or with pebbles. Less expensive still and very easy to construct, a rolled-steel joist (RSJ) or iron girder placed on its side and sunk in the ground can be used as the water carrier. If the rill is in a part of the garden that does not have a formal presence, say, in long grass, you might line the base with pebbles and allow it to rust.

A rill can follow the natural incline of a garden on a slope and, if the area is large enough, might wind its way around the trunks of a group of trees, or follow a serpentine route to fall into a pool, then travel on to drop into another pool beyond. To capture the

energy of movement, you can create a disturbance in the water surface by chiselling grooves into the stone on the bottom of the rill, or play a more elaborate game with it and have chiselled-out runs followed by smooth runs, so that you get a rhythm that is alternately agitated then calm. Situations such as these presuppose moving water, and if you are fortunate enough to have a natural spring within the garden, this will be the ideal way to feed the rill. But it is not difficult to fit a pump to circulate the water, although I think it is important to have one that can be kept on continuously – switching your rill on and off by hand does little to sustain the desired illusion.

A beautiful way to use a rill of still water is to have it crossing an area of grass, perhaps separating long grass from mown, or bordering an area of wild flower grass. In this context it would give the best effect if the grass were to grow right up to the sides of the rill, so that lawn and water merge seamlessly.

In the same way, a perfectly square lawn could be exquisitely framed by having a narrow rill that runs around the four sides and is then planted up with water iris in each of the corners. Or, it might be that a sheltered corner of a very large lawn is separated from the rest by a curved rill entirely planted with iris, except for one small gap that becomes the entrance to this enchanted island. With a table and chairs, it becomes an intimate enclosure, reached only by crossing the water. Many Lutyens and Jekyll gardens were designed with stone rills planted with water lilies or kingcups. Taking inspiration from this, you could make a small rill that forms a border along one side of the terrace of a small town garden and have it planted with miniature water lilies.

Canals are larger than rills and usually rectangular. These large, still bodies of water can be used to introduce an atmosphere of calm formality in a garden. On the right kind of ground, they are not necessarily expensive features to make, and if a garden is on heavy clay, then digging out a canal is no different from digging out a natural pond as the clay will hold the water naturally. If the garden is large enough, you may also be able to use the resulting spoil heap for land sculpture elsewhere. In gardens on non-clay soils, a heavy butyl liner, of the kind used for agricultural reservoirs, will need to be used to retain the water, but it is not difficult to mould the liner to shape; in fact, it is generally easier to make these formal shapes than it is to simulate the look of a natural body of water. A canal might be quite a grand

ABOVE In this contemporary scheme, the lawns appear as floating pads of green between ribbons of water. The water could be planted up with water iris to create a semi-transparent surface and make a contrast to the grass.

BELOW Within this formal modern pool, the concentric circles introduce a sculptural element that also creates neat divisions between the different types of water planting.

affair, some 20 or 30m (65 or 98ft) long by 10m (33ft) wide, or it might be midway between a rill and a canal, say, 20m (65ft) long and 1.5m (5ft) wide, with box cloud-shaped hedging on either side of it, or just lawn coming up to the edges.

Water is an endlessly valuable tool for bringing both calm and energy into a garden and you can use its opposing qualities for different effects. It is always enchanting to linger near water, to sit and watch it. The way that water reflects light will add spontaneous movement at certain times of the day. Still water draws extra attention to any feature reflected in it: trees, architecture, statuary, a piece of modern sculpture or simply a beautiful piece of driftwood. Water is also a life force and a life-giver: it brings wildlife into the garden, and it is instinctive to want

to include its movement and energy within the garden whenever possible, even if the scale is small.

In a small garden, the serenity of a still, circular pool might be energized by a fountain or by a single spout of water that comes up and breaks the surface of the water. A tiny courtyard, with glass doors opening onto it from the house, could be almost filled by a big square or rectangle of dark water that is bordered by paving and a line of pleached lime trees. You could perhaps install a header tank on the roof that supplies a gravity-fed fountain in the pool. Only when it rains, the fountain will send a metre-high jet of water into the air, lasting as long as the reserve of water. No technical expertise is needed to create this fantastic water trick, and your still pool constantly replenished with fresh water in an environmentally friendly way.

HORIZONTALS

101

NATURAL WATER

ALL OF NATURE'S WATER FEATURES — PONDS, STREAMS
and rivers, even the sea — come within the range of
horizontal elements in a garden. Where they occur
naturally, they enhance the surroundings enormously,
but, apart from a pond, which can be made to look
natural and wild relatively easily, I would never
suggest trying to re-create them.

If you are lucky enough to have a stream or small
river running through your garden, your main job
will be to respect it by nurturing and sustaining its
health, and to manage it by taking out invasive plants,

FAR LEFT The cultivated and the wild merge beautifully here, with native grasses and reeds growing at the water's furthest edges, while water lilies flourish on the surface.

BELOW This small river is allowed to retain its natural character at its margins, making the contrast with the garden environment even more dramatic.

and clearing nettles and weeds away from its edges. The qualities of naturally moving water can be enhanced in a very non-invasive way, either by creating a small dam at one end of a stream with some timber planking or by placing some large tree trunks across it, which will subtly alter the movement and the sound of the water.

You may need to decide how the rest of the garden will connect with this area of moving water. Should the grass around it be left to grow long or should it be mown and kept short? Should you give some

protection to the banks by putting in a wooden edge? Do you plant its banks with water iris and, if the water is wide enough, how should you bridge it if it lies entirely within your boundaries? If it constitutes a boundary in itself, how can you use it to your visual advantage? When a stream crosses the garden in a more dramatic way, you will need to give some thought as to how to incorporate it into the overall design for your garden.

Natural ponds and pools need to sit in the landscape as you would expect to find them in nature – nestled in a dip where water would naturally gather or in a hollow that might be filled by a stream. Ponds don't have to be huge – something that is 6 x 10m (20 x 33ft) or even 6 x 6m (20 x 20ft) can look perfectly natural. On heavy clay soils, the cavity can simply be dug out and the water will be retained naturally. On lighter soils, you might choose to use the traditional method of puddling. This involves smoothing over the whole of the inner surface of the pond with clay to make it watertight. This is how most village ponds on non-clay soils would have been made in the days before butyl liners, and there is indeed something very pleasing about making a pond in this earthy and organic way.

Most ponds these days are lined with a liner cut to fit the shape and size of the pond. The most critical part is disguising the edge of the liner: you need to make sure that it is securely buried under the ground so that grass can come right up to the pond margins and merge in with the water plants. With careful attention to detail in the planting, the pond should then look completely natural.

SWIMMING POOLS

THE DECISION TO INCLUDE A SWIMMING POOL IN THE garden requires careful consideration, particularly in climates where it is unlikely to be used all year round: where best to site it, how to enclose it, what materials it should be built in and what, if any, colours should be used? The stereotypical bright blue mosaic-tiled pool, which we are all preconditioned to think of, really does not work in the garden environment, as it creates too much of a visual shock. There are many more beautiful ways to make a pool that fits in with its surroundings, and which will probably cost much less, too.

For me, a swimming pool should be rectangular, a big *bassin* like a Roman bath, never kidney-shaped. The inside of the pool could be simply painted or tiled; if you have the budget, it could be tiled in stone, or leaving the grey render unpainted will turn the pool a soft blue-green on sunny days, while in winter it will merge naturally with the garden surroundings. Neutral colours, like stone and beige or soft aqua-greens tend to work best, but before choosing paint or coloured tiles, do some research or get professional advice on how different colours react to water – the depth of water will subtly alter the colour, as will sunshine on a hot day or cloud on a grey day.

Dark pools have their own particular magic. A black-painted pool, with its invisible depths, can be used to make a strong architectural impact, although its appeal is not for everyone. The pool at Hatfield House in Hertfordshire is painted a gorgeous dark aubergine and has a yew maze as its backdrop; swimming in it is like swimming in ink. For an entirely different look, stainless steel makes a beautiful contemporary pool – sleek and brilliant, but expensive.

ABOVE This long canal pool has a dry-stone wall at one end that appears to continue under the water. Its stone interior takes on many different colours, depending on the weather. Here, in the sun, it is a beautiful aqua-blue.

FAR LEFT Sited within the walls of a tumbledown building, this pool is protected and secluded, with an atmosphere of romance that an open space would lack.

As important as the pool itself is the pool edge and surround. Too often an expensive mosaic-tiled pool is ruined by an ugly precast concrete edge. One of the most important considerations is the scale and size of the edge. Stone, granite or brick all make good alternatives. A band of stone around the pool edge can be taken down the sides and about 30cm (12in) into the water, so that it merges with the tiles or render. Decking makes a beautiful pool edge, going right up to the water. Use a big substantial timber around the edge to keep the planks in place, and let it all bleach out, like the deck of a ship.

The dramatic visual impact that a well-sited weir pool or infinity pool can make speaks for itself by allowing a seamless fusion with the surrounding landscape. Even if this type of construction is beyond your budget, have the water level come as close as possible to the top of the pool edge, so that you have the sensation of becoming part of the garden when you are in the pool. The alternative is swimming down in a hole with no view out and only walls to look at.

Most outdoor pools are built for family and friends to have fun in, rather than for serious exercise; their function is social and they need to be an aesthetic part of the garden. Something often overlooked is the fact that pool accessories made of coloured plastic are largely unattractive and tend to ruin the overall appearance, there are alternatives in more sympathetic materials. Pool covers, too, can completely overwhelm and are hugely expensive items. Although they are needed as a safety measure, particularly for children, and to conserve heat, you should do your research carefully to make sure you have not overlooked a solution that would be more aesthetically pleasing.

Keeping the pool in sympathy with its surroundings is important but difficult. The best advice is to keep the whole thing as simple as possible. There is no need for acres of paving around the pool; having grass coming up to the pool edge is nicer underfoot and, in a country garden, more appropriate. If you don't want to go for a conventional chemical pool, you might opt instead for a saline or ozone pool.

One of my favourite swimming pools is set in the dappled shade of trees within a little dry-stone walled garden with cow parsley growing around it. The owners simply dug a hole, laid breeze blocks one on top of the other, covered it with a black pool liner and put an oak surround around the edge. At one end there is an old stone mounting block with a mask that spits water into the pool; there's no pump – the water gets topped up with a hose whenever necessary, and an occasional glass of chlorine is just chucked into it. This is about as uncomplicated and unpretentious as it gets.

Does a swimming pool have to be a swimming pool in the conventional sense at all? Pools are for play and for cooling down on a hot day, so why not go back to the seventeenth- and eighteenth-century dipping pools that were made purely for plunging into, as a means of invigorating body and soul. A deep, octagonal pool of water in a shaded part of the garden could be a refreshing dipping place on hot days.

A swimming pool does need to be sheltered from the wind. Walls can make the whole environment seem very harsh and, unless you have a natural enclosure of trees, the best way to surround a pool is with hedging. A modern pool with a deck of chunky oak planks could be set within a thick band of green, either beech or box cloud-shaped hedging, with some blue agapanthus in containers, or two or three large square containers filled with water lilies.

BELOW This is the ultimate natural swimming pool. Within the planted pool, there is a basin kept clear of plants. The water is kept clean by having the right balance of plants and filtering it through a series of mini-reed beds. There is no need for chemicals or artificial colour.

In a larger garden, where the pool is some way from the house, a small building is a worthwhile addition for storing a table and chairs, some plates, glasses and cutlery for impromptu meals. Add a small fridge for cool drinks, and the experience of spending a hot summer's day by the pool is complete.

Another alternative to a conventional swimming pool would be a natural pool, in which plants, rather than chemicals, are used to maintain the natural balance and keep the water clean. This method mimics the natural environment of lakes and ponds, with their marginal planting of reeds and aquatic plants. The pool may be made of concrete and the area for planting separated from the swimming area by a low wall under the water level. This kind of swimming pool looks good at all times of year, and allows the experience of swimming in an environment that looks and feels entirely natural.

punctuation

BELOW LEFT Punctuation points within the garden need not always be solid objects. These wonderful spheres of bent hazel create an ephemeral sculpture, which, although it might last only a few seasons, can easily be made again.

BELOW CENTRE Fountains and other water features can create a strong focus in the garden, used either at the beginning, the middle or the end of a particular area.

This section of the book deals with the features and structures that act as focal points within the garden: the garden buildings, seating areas, pergolas, arches, fountains, sculptures and plant supports. Punctuation covers the all-important signposts that draw the visitor through the garden. The presence and positioning of punctuation bring a sense of purpose to the design by offering a destination or a pause on the journey, an opportunity to make a choice of routes or to sit and rest.

At a meeting point between paths, a sculpture or stone basin with water spilling over its rim might be used to arrest the attention of the visitor and provide a pause to consider which path to take. Halfway down a long path, a bench placed in the niche of a hedge offers a place to rest and look around, to enjoy the planting in an adjacent bed, and to look back and see the view from an entirely new perspective. Seating has many functions in the garden environment. Sometimes it can

be used artfully: a chair in a wild flower meadow has a kind of poetry about it, but poses the question of whether it is really meant for sitting in or will the grasses and flowers be squashed. Areas set up permanently for table and chairs are among the most used spaces in the garden, and the choice of furniture, as well as the ambience it evokes, will influence the way these areas are used.

Garden buildings are hugely influential elements of garden punctuation. Their beauty is that they extend the time and seasons during which the garden can be enjoyed. Not everyone can have the luxury of a garden pavilion or an outhouse, but it is quite possible to design and build something new and interesting out of recycled and reclaimed materials. And, as anyone who has a greenhouse will know, the pleasures afforded by the smallest space for sowing and growing can be among the most satisfying that the garden has to offer.

BELOW Gardens are not complete without somewhere to sit, relax and reflect on our journey through them. Benches need to be things of beauty, and their comfort (or lack of it) may play an important part in how long you wish the traveller to rest before moving on.

These beautiful sculptures, shaped like giant molluscs, have been carved from solid lumps of wood. They not only punctuate and decorate the garden environment, but also double up as informal seats. Their organic shapes make a satisfying cluster on an open area of lawn, and invite closer inspection.

Water soothes and lifts the spirits. An energetic plume of water introduces a dynamic vertical focus into the garden and creates around it a place to pause and reflect. In an urban environment, the sound of water can be an effective device for covering up the drone of traffic and other unwanted noises.

The water in this pool pours gently into a rectangular basin from a simple spout. An uncluttered design like this would be ideal for a small town or courtyard garden, where it could be adapted in many ways. This pool has been made of stone, but it could be built from brick or even concrete for a very modern look.

A waterfall runs down the side of a 'staircase' jutting out of a wall. The water chutes are four sections of rusted iron girder, which make a wonderful contrast with the natural stone wall. A feature like this could be small and self-contained, or part of a larger feature, with the water falling into a rill or pool.

Moss has been allowed to cover the bowl of this beautiful fountain. The jet of water punctuates the surface, and the whole effect is sensual, calm and cool. It would be equally magical in a shady courtyard with orange trees and box balls, or standing alone in a swathe of green lawn.

FOUNTAINS, SCULPTURE

There is a grandeur about this stone figure spurting water out of a trumpet that suggests formality, but its setting could be traditional or modern. The figure could be used as the one exciting baroque detail in a minimalist garden, standing at the end of a long rectangular pool.

Animal heads on four sides of this Renaissance-style fountain bowl spout water into a pool below. The water could equally well be made to fall into a shallow cobbled basin, where the water drains away between the stones, making the splashing sound even more dramatic.

A pitted stone ball sits on a mossy wall, looking as though it has been there forever. A ball such as this could be used singly or as one of a series placed along a wall to punctuate its length or, perhaps, to mark a particular point, such as where a staircase begins.

113

FOUNTAINS

THE DECORATIVE EFFECT OF FOUNTAINS AND OTHER water features is their most obvious attraction, but perhaps more important is their role in bringing movement to a garden. The movement of the water itself transforms a static space with its energy, and draws people towards it, generating even more movement around it.

Whether it is water brimming over a huge urn or a small bubbling spring, a sleek and contemporary installation or a traditional and mossy piece of stonework, each fountain is a kind of punctuation mark. A small bubble fountain might act as a pause or a comma as you walk from one part of the garden to another. A wall fountain placed at the end of a long walkway creates an axis that draws you along the path and acts as a full stop – the finale for that part of the garden. A fountain placed at the intersection of paths becomes a question mark as you ask yourself which path you should now take.

ABOVE This simple wooden spout lined with lead allows the water to pour gently into the trough below. A detail like this is perfectly suited to a hot, sunny courtyard, bringing coolness and a sense of tranquillity to the space.

FAR RIGHT These dancing plumes of water contrast beautifully with the still calm canal at their centre. The entire environment is one of misty seduction.

Fountains can be powerful and volatile or barely moving and gentle. The Emperor Fountain at Chatsworth House in Derbyshire, though impossibly grand in scale for an ordinary garden, has an energy about it that could act as inspiration for a small space that needs movement and stimulation: you might have a single jet of water rising 2m (6½ft) into the air, then splashing back down onto a surface that is shallowly dished and paved in stone or cobbles.

The energy of water draws people and makes it a highly interactive element. In a large space, a series of jets that hurtle up into the air and blow around on a windy day before splashing back down again onto the stone invite play: you can walk between the jets, but will you get wet?

These high-energy fountains command attention and create a distraction from whatever else is going on. They work in public spaces, but in a garden it is better to be able to vary the mood. A valve system that operates to moderate the flow and turn it right down to the smallest bubble jet will give you the option of choosing the kind of punctuation you want within the space at any time. In a small garden enclosure, you might have a fountain contained within a pool so that water falls back into water. If it is operated by a sensor, in the same way as a security light, the moment that someone walks into the space, the pump will be switched on and darts of water will spring up as if by magic. If the sensor is also connected to a timer, the fountain might be set to stay on only for a minute and stop as suddenly as it started.

In a shady courtyard, a more naturalistic feature might be appropriate, with water trickling down onto rocks and stones piled up around the fountain. If the

rocks are tufa or soft limestone, then at their edges, away from the main action of the water, the perpetual dampness will gradually allow the rocks to become colonized by mosses and ferns, just as they would be at the margins of a waterfall. Where something gentle and mysterious is preferred, a mist fountain could be installed so, instead of a jet of water, a very fine spray catches the light and makes rainbows in the sun. The constant moisture in the atmosphere will gradually result in mosses and ferns growing in the crevices between the surrounding stones, creating a stone and water garden that is peaceful and green.

Staddlestones are usually limestone or sandstone, and good vehicles for water. A single stone, drilled through and set on a terrace, could just have water barely bubbling up over it, wetting only part of the stone. Or a modern version could be made out of a drilled cube with a small bowl carved into it, so that the water wells up first before flowing over the stone. This would also make a place for the birds to come and drink, bringing more life into the garden.

Water dripping or pouring downwards creates a different type of effect. The most striking fountains can be the ones that deliver the unexpected. At Parnham House in Dorset, there is a huge mask that spits water into a trough. The water then continues down a pair of rills and on into the lake. The energy of the water as it splashes down grabs your attention, but when you look into the trough, you find that it is empty and that the water never stops moving but continually passes straight through it. This awakens your curiosity and prompts you to look for the path of the water and follow it through its course until it ends up in the lake.

ABOVE At the centre of my own garden, this urn spits water into a circular pool. Positioned where four paths meet, the urn sets up four new axis points, offering the visitor a choice of routes.

FAR RIGHT An old-fashioned garden sprinkler has been used to create a fountain in a natural pond. The pressure of the water spins the nozzles to form dancing spirals of water that catch the light.

In a wall-mounted fountain, the water might pour through a spout or slide out through a narrow slit in the wall, instead of the usual lion's head or other kind of mask. Or it could emerge from a rusty pipe or an old RSJ fixed on its side as a shute to send water down into a pool. Water can pour over stainless steel or glass; this idea might be used to make a dramatic tall screen that acts as a division between one part of the garden and another. In a long, narrow town garden, a wall of steel and water two-thirds of the way down its length might mark the transition from sunny flower garden to tree-dappled shade, reflecting indistinctly the warm colours of flowers on one side, the shadowy greens on the other. Lighting, in conjunction with this kind of water screen, could be used to great effect to create a diversion within a garden at night and block out views beyond your boundaries.

The sound that water makes – crashing, splashing or dripping – adds another dimension, which can sometimes be used specifically to tune out the constant hum of traffic in a town garden or even to create a kind of musical notation. For our 'Evolution' garden at the 2000 Chelsea Flower Show, Piet Oudolf and I had large, empty stainless-steel bowls and a water device that sent the water hopping from one bowl to another. As the water jet hit the bowls, it rang out, almost like a bell, making a kind of music.

The playfulness of water makes it an endlessly fascinating element to use. In the clearing of a woodland garden, you might have a little pool covered with duckweed and in it a fountain with a spray pattern, like an old-fashioned sprinkler. The water spins upwards in a spiral and falls back into the pool, forming a perfect circle on the green surface.

SCULPTURE

ANY AESTHETIC OBJECT IN THE GARDEN, WHETHER A
stone figure, an abstract carving or a curiously shaped
piece of wood can constitute a sculpture, but the real
art is in the placing of it. With skill you can add
something to the space: a sense of grandeur, a surprise
or just a talking point.

A particular piece of sculpture may be chosen and
placed to dominate a space or to act as a centrepoint;
alternatively, a smaller, more subtle piece may serve
to enhance an area of planting by unveiling itself
only when you are close up. In a large garden, a
series of objects might be carefully placed to lead
you through the space, with each piece inviting you
to touch and interact, and adding its individual
contribution to the various locations. In a smaller
garden, a sculpture may serve to extend the view.
By placing it at the furthest extreme of the garden
or even by finding a way to have it outside your
boundaries, perhaps in a neighbouring field, you will
extend the perceived space.

Using sculpture in any of these ways adds another
layer of interest and helps introduce a sense of scale
into the garden; in a large open area without any
recognizable reference points, a single piece or a
group of sculptures could be used to help make sense
of the space. As sculpture can be used to orientate, so
it can be used to disorientate: all sorts of tricks can be
played with size and distance to add an element of
intrigue in the garden.

Placing sculpture within the garden is rather like
hanging pictures in a room. The pieces you choose
and the way you decide to display them can be used
to bring about a variety of different effects, either to
harmonize with the surroundings or to provoke a

LEFT Certain types of sculpture
gain from subtle positioning.
These intriguing wooden figures,
placed among trees, create a
delightful surprise when
discovered; the act of stumbling
upon them as you wander around
the garden gives them a greater
sense of power and importance
than when seen from a distance.

TOP RIGHT A modern installation
of airy glass seed heads set in a
meadow draws us nearer so that
we can examine their beauty in
closer detail.

BOTTOM RIGHT The shadows
that this sculpture casts create
a secondary art form. They make
an ever-shifting pattern on the
ground that changes shape and
size according to the time of day
and the season.

reaction. Beautiful urns or classical statuary placed formally in niches or flanking entrances perform a role that we would now define as traditional in the garden. They complement the planted structure of the garden and play the part of ornament, offering a vocabulary that is familiar to us from eighteenth-century gardens. We can borrow from the vocabulary but bring it up to date by reintroducing the element of surprise that these objects would once have produced. So a modern colonnade could be made from a long run of hedge that has niches carved into it at intervals, in which you house a series of contemporary urns.

Sculptures do not have to be expensive any more than they have to be original bought pieces. If you have an old urn or even a fragment of one, you might build a fanciful column from reclaimed bricks on

LEFT The placing of urns is not as easy as one might suppose, but this classic limestone urn fits very comfortably into the corner junction between two rows of pleached hornbeams.

ABOVE This sculptural installation of hoops crossing the water is given life and movement by the jets of water that hop between and around them – they also introduce sound and humour.

which to display it. You might make your own sculptural artworks from natural raw materials: a collection of flints stacked into a column, an old tree trunk carved into an obelisk, a totem pole of wood, painted in rich colours.

The simplest objects can make an impact: a clutch of large stone or wooden balls scattered over a lawn, for example, look as though they have just been cast there by the hand of a giant. Outsize stone 'seed pods' lying beneath the trees in a woodland area add form to the tangle of undergrowth and take the place of flowers. These objects add a note of humour; they can be moved around and rearranged at whim.

Sculptural containers can also be used to define and reinforce areas, such as the edge of a terrace. By placing a line or a group of containers at the threshold between grass and paving, you add weight and point out where the contained garden ends and the garden proper begins.

Whenever pots and containers are being used to perform the role of sculpture, simplicity is the key. If a pot has a strong architectural form, it can almost certainly stand on its own; the elegant lines of a beautifully textured modern ceramic jar will bring a sense of calm to a terraced area, and no planting is needed to improve it.

The style of pots and the way in which they are planted should be kept very simple. The strongest impact comes from using a single specimen like an agave or a clipped box ball that is in itself sculptural, or one type of plant, say, a profusion of flax blue plumbago instead of a mass of various flowering plants.

People often assume that small spaces need small objects, when actually the reverse is true. Even in the smallest of courtyard gardens or terraces, it is more effective to have just one very large or three medium-sized pots in the same style than a welter of small pots of different shapes and colours. A jumble of pots makes the space seem smaller, because the eye is constantly hopping from one to another, unable to find a focus or a place to rest. Instead, imagine the impact in a small city courtyard of a large contemporary container made of steel or granite that is simply filled with water and planted with the linear forms of water iris or a stand of bulrushes. A statement like this, bold and simple, can make the ordinary seem extraordinary.

An unpainted wooden bench can become more beautiful as it takes on the patina of age. The soft grey-green of this lichen-covered bench allows it to sit comfortably and naturally within its environment.

In this town garden, the seating area is integral to the planting, allowing one to be in direct contact with the plants.

This serpentine bench wraps itself around the tree providing places to sit, either leaning against the trunk or so that two people can sit facing each other, in the style of a traditional love seat.

A seat can be used purely as a punctuation point in the garden. Long grass growing through the slats of this elegant seat gives it an air of light-hearted romance.

A covered timber seat adds a note of eccentricity to a wild part of the garden, and offers a comfortable shelter from which to observe and be part of the natural setting.

SEATING AREAS

An air of relaxed informality surrounds these worn and sagging benches and table, suggesting that they are probably often used for impromptu dining.

SEATING AREAS

THERE SHOULD ALWAYS BE AT LEAST ONE PLACE IN THE
garden where you can sit and relax: a place for quiet
contemplation, somewhere to sit around a table with
friends and enjoy a glass of wine or a delicious meal.
These areas are a vital part of the garden environment,
and their sole function is to offer a place to stop and
take pleasure in the garden.

In small gardens, the seating area is usually the main
terrace where there may be a table and chairs
permanently set out. In larger gardens, an al fresco
eating area will, for convenience, probably be close to
the house, but there may also be two or three other
spots that make natural pausing places. It would be
useful to have a seat, for example, on a path alongside
a flower border, in the corner of a working kitchen
garden or simply in a spot that enjoys the last rays of
the evening sun. These small resting places need not

ABOVE It is always convenient
to have a table and chairs that can
be moved from one place in the
garden to another. Here, bringing
the chairs out into a meadow
allows you to enjoy the natural
world on a fine summer's day.

RIGHT A series of different-sized
wooden cubes form subdivisions
and give added structure to this
garden space, while also doubling
up usefully as seats.

FAR RIGHT In this Italian
garden, an old table and chairs
make an outdoor dining room for
spontaneous entertaining, giving
added purpose to the space.

necessarily be formalized. In a wild or woodland area of the garden, the seat might be simply a fallen tree trunk or a rough structure made of two or three rustic poles nailed to sturdy timber uprights – a place to perch for a while.

Garden furniture falls into two distinct groups: the fixed and the movable. A seat might become a permanent feature by virtue of the fact that it is too heavy to be moved around, or that it forms part of the architecture of the garden, such as a little wall niche with a roof and built-in seat.

Details such as these add character and introduce an element of intimacy, and it is important that the materials used should be in sympathy with the style and atmosphere of the garden. A seat built into a wall might be a stone slab that picks up on the stone of the wall, or a sturdy oak plank supported by simple

ABOVE This beautiful construction of logs combines a wall and a seat, with the cantilevered poles at the base providing support for the long low bench that seems to float from the wall.

wooden uprights, or it might be something more ornate, like a beautiful Edwardian cast-iron bench that just fits snugly into the recess.

In addition to its practical purpose, a beautifully crafted seat can also be a piece of sculpture. An old curved iron seat may have a hornbeam arbour shaped like a quarter-sphere planted around it. The seat becomes part of the planting, and the two materials appear to grow into one another. In the same way, a timber seat built around a tree adorns the tree, as well as giving distinction to it.

The social and conversational function of seating is paramount in these comfortable curving shapes that bring people close together. The curling 'S' shape of the love seat, like the yin and yang symbol, brings form and function together perfectly with economy of line. A variant on this, simpler still, might be a backless timber seat, placed so that two people can sit beside each other, facing opposite directions, to enjoy an intimate conversation.

What constitutes a seat? It might not be instantly recognizable as such, but a pile of logs in the right position or a low run of dry-stone walling given a turf or camomile top make unusual organic seats in dry weather. They form an integral part of the garden's character, and we have the sensation as we

LEFT The curved seat on this
roof terrace has been elevated
above the decking. By keeping
the number of different materials
to a minimum, the design is both
pleasing and harmonious.

BELOW Two simple metal
trestles have been used as the
supports for a thick plank table
top. Not only is the table used
for outdoor meals, but it is also
the base for a 'tablescape'.

RIGHT Placed casually on a jetty, movable campaign chairs offer comfortable seating for the observation of wild life in and around the pond. Their neutral colours preserve the tranquillity of the scene.

FAR RIGHT Plain timber seats and a table that suit the setting perfectly prove that outdoor furniture can be both functional and good-looking without costing a huge amount of money.

perch on them that we, too, have become part of the garden at that moment. Other kinds of incidental seats might be carved stone balls or wooden seed pods distributed like punctuation points among humps of box on a lawn.

Alongside these fixed structures are the comparative lightweights – the movable pieces that can be picked up and carried to different places. A balance of furniture that stays and pieces that move usually brings out the best in a garden.

According to taste and preference, the movable pieces of garden furniture might be made of wirework, light metal or wood. Regency game and barrow seats were made with wheels, so that they could be manoeuvred easily around the garden; these styles of seat are still made today. As well as being comfortable and practical, the furniture needs to sit

well within the design of the garden. In a garden that is rambling and informal, a mismatched set of old deckchairs with faded fabric seats will look completely at home, but in a very contemporary garden, you might choose to have some modern deckchairs or a zinc-topped table on the terrace.

A few comfortable sun-loungers beside a swimming pool are perfect for stretching out on for a snooze after an energetic swim. These could vary in style from Edwardian-style teak steamer chairs or, at the other end of the scale, very modern swivel-loungers that are fixed to the deck and can turn through 360 degrees to follow the sun. As part of my design for a garden in France, a series of sculpted oak daybeds, based on my interpretation of a design by Mies van der Rohe, is arranged in a line down the side of the pool.

Creating a living willow dome is not as difficult as it might appear. Long willow whips, pushed into the ground to form a circle, have rooted and produced shoots. These are held together by a series of concentric rings woven into the structure, which become progressively smaller as they reach the top.

This temporary structure of hazel poles is simply tied together at the top to form a wigwam – the ideal support for scrambling scented sweet peas.

Pergolas offer an alternative way to view and experience plants, allowing us to walk beneath the canopy of their leaves and stems, and appreciate flowers at close quarters.

PERGOLAS, ARCHES, PLANT SUPPORTS

These hornbeam arches entice you to follow their winding route. The wide spacing between them lets you see out and lets light in, making it possible for plants to grow around and beneath the structure.

Rustic timber is a very quick and inexpensive material for a beautiful screen, with endless opportunities for varying the pattern. The latticework here becomes the perfect support for a vigorous climbing rose

PERGOLAS

PART PLANTED STRUCTURE, PART GARDEN BUILDING,
pergolas contribute a strong architectural presence to
a garden. Their main purpose is to link one part of the
garden with another, providing height and structure.
The scale and design of the pergola may range from
an extensive colonnaded walkway built in a mix of
timber, stone and brick to a simple timber-only
construction, but the framework always acts as a
support system for the climbing plants that clothe it.
The beauty of these structures lies in their three-
dimensionality: from outside, they offer the visual
spectacle of a building made of plants; from inside,
there is the pleasurable sensation of walking under a
roof of green, with the fragrance of rose or jasmine,
the dripping trails of wisteria or clusters of ripening
grapes all around you.

The Edwardians developed and refined the pergola,
turning it into a form of garden art. The device
appears frequently in Lutyens and Jekyll gardens,

RIGHT Plant and structure have
become one in this pergola of
trained Judas trees. The passage
of time has made the original
supports redundant, and the
blossom-covered branches have
taken on their role.

taking the traveller between one garden section and another, or linking the house and terrace with a pool. The grander examples were constructed with stone or brick columns supporting a structure of horizontal timber crossbeams and sometimes featured flagstone floors. They might be planted with a mixture of roses, wisteria, jasmine and vines or, sometimes, with a single plant, such as wisteria or the same species of rose.

These period structures show the simple system of verticals and horizontals given endless variation with the choice of columns, which might be classical, turned wood, square, round or octagonal, square brick piers or round stone columns.

The roof of a pergola is usually flat, and the overhead structure of horizontal timber beams can be interpreted in a number of different ways. The timbers may be plain or may have other timbers crossing them. They may be fixed closely together to allow the planting to cover the structure densely or be more widely spaced to allow sunlight in. Sometimes, in a long run, it is possible to vary the rhythm, so that closely spaced beams give way to an open section, where the pergola changes direction or a path crosses the structure. Occasionally, at the beginning or the middle of a run, the timbers can rise to form a pointed roof, allowing the climbers to clamber up high into the light, or the whole structure may be designed as a pair of square, walled pavilions that are connected by a walkway.

A pergola made entirely of timber will tend to be less dominating, but can still be quite a robust structure. The degree of formality needed depends on the context. A pergola built in an Arts and Crafts

LEFT The twisted stems of the vine are supported by a rustic wooden structure that does not overwhelm the character of the plant, but allows the landscape to be the dominant feature.

RIGHT In this formal vegetable garden, a wide and elegant metal tunnel becomes the perfect support for various annual climbers, from pumpkins through to sweet peas and runner beans.

style of beautifully tenoned and mortised timbers would make a perfect choice for a house and garden of that period, particularly if the structure is close to the house and terrace. A pergola further from the house, in a more relaxed or working part of the garden, might take its cue from the immediate environment and use rustic pine timber with the bark still in place or even pieces of driftwood to make a free-form organic structure.

Trellis-framed pergolas have an elegance and lightness about them that might suit a walled town garden that needs a certain amount of formality. A structure like this will also create privacy, screening views into the garden from overlooking buildings and making a semi-covered area where it is pleasant to sit among the plants.

In a hot climate a vine-clad timber pergola that runs around three walls of a courtyard creates welcome dappled shade. It can be connected to the walls, rather than be freestanding, to form a leafy cloistered walkway. The degree of shade created by a pergola might not be suitable for a small garden in a cooler climate, but in gardens that are already shady, a pergola can be used to support and grow plants that might otherwise fail, by lifting them up into the light.

Modern pergolas made of steel with high-tensile wire stretched between the verticals have the advantage of airiness and transparency. In a contemporary garden, these materials could be used to construct a non-invasive plant frame that spans a considerable distance or extends high above the garden without seeming to dominate it.

ARCHES

Simple metal arches clad in climbing roses make perfect punctuation points in an exuberant herbaceous garden, bringing in the required height and helping guide visitors through the space.

RIGHT In a semi-wild and informal setting, this metal arch requires no plants. Its clean and simple lines create a perfect balance between nature and the man-made.

FRAMING ENTRANCES, STEPS AND PATHS, ARCHES OFFER a controlled way of introducing height to the garden. A well-placed arch will lead the eye onwards, especially if it supports a fine array of climbing plants.

The growth habit of flowering climbers, including many roses, clematis and some honeysuckles, suits this type of support well, and helps show plants off to their best advantage. It is much easier to reach plants for pruning and tying in when they are climbing an arch than when they are supported by a large wall, and it is a good method of disciplining and keeping vigorous climbers within bounds.

In its simplest form, an arch might simply be made from bent hazel rods pushed into the ground and woven together at the top to make an informal, cottage-garden support for annual climbers of all kinds, from runner beans and sweet peas to ornamental gourds.

Although we usually think of an arch as being a curved structure, the crosspiece can, in fact, be square. A square arch made of rustic timber with the bark still attached makes a charming and unpretentious prop for climbing plants, productive and flowering, from grapevines to trachelospermum.

This kind of square-topped structure is very simple to make, by fixing pairs of horizontal posts to the top of the pairs of verticals on either side that are sunk in the ground. The wider the span, the more structured the arch needs to be, but the supporting details can become part of the arch's decoration.

Wirework and galvanized structures are light and airy, and their transparency makes them a good choice where nothing too dominating is required. They add a form of three-dimensional patterning and add a layer of intricacy to the garden in winter when it is bare of leaves. The metalwork can be left to weather or be painted a colour. It can be effective to mix materials: wooden posts, for example, can have a metal arch fixed into them to make the overhead span.

Opportunities for pattern-making can be extended by arranging the arches themselves into a formation. For example, a formally laid-out kitchen garden with four paths meeting in the centre, might have an arch at the start of each path and, at the point where the paths converge, four arches crossing over from corner to corner to make a central vaulted arch.

Illustrations of medieval gardens show that arches were used extensively and sometimes sprang from walls to make cloistered walks. This would translate easily to a small walled garden where half-arches can be fixed on to one of the walls at intervals, forming a framework that is at once a structure to support climbers and an inviting walkway.

Mixing the formal with the informal can produce magical results. There can be nothing more beautiful to look at and to walk through than a series of arches, crossing a wild flower meadow, planted up with magnificently fragrant old roses.

PUNCTUATION

PLANT SUPPORTS

THE ESSENCE OF A GOOD PLANT SUPPORT IS THAT IT
should secure the plant firmly and neatly in a way that
also benefits the plant. At home I use hazel to make
big, hooped upturned 'baskets' as supports for the long
lax stems of old-fashioned roses. Wherever the stem is
bent over and tied in, the rose shoots from the apex,
and hundreds more flowers are produced, turning the
whole thing into a flowering ball.

There are many other beautiful and inexpensive
ways to make natural plant supports, from twiggy
pea-sticks fixed in the ground for annual climbers
to scramble over to home-made hazel wigwams for
sweet peas, runner beans, even clematis. The main
appeal of these props is their impermanence, and their

simple and rustic appearance is right for country
gardens or annual borders, vegetable and herb plots.

The design and choice of materials will be
influenced by the style of planting and the overall
look that you want. Wrought-iron structures are
traditional supports, particularly for roses, and can
look very elegant in formal gardens, especially when
used as a form of medium-height punctuation within
borders. Pyramids or other shapes of painted or rusty
metal will dress down the formality of the material
and fit in with a more relaxed style of planting.

Old stone columns in a border make wonderful
architectural supports for climbing roses, but not
everyone is lucky enough to have such a feature.

FAR LEFT When using
metalwork to support plants,
I prefer not to paint it, but to
allow the metal to rust so that
it blends in with the natural
earth tones of the garden.

LEFT Plant supports are
sometimes used purely as
temporary structures, as with
this arbour of apples. Once
the trees have established and
matured, they will become
naturally self-supporting.

At the other extreme, a heavy wooden post makes an uncomplicated support to suit any kind of climber. Columns of sturdy trelliswork, painted or unpainted, add an element of theatricality and make attractive climbing frames for a collection of old-fashioned shrub or climbing roses. By contrast, you might make a very contemporary structure using steel with high-tensile wires, or have four oak posts set closely to create a column, with wire between them on which the climber is trained.

To work effectively as punctuation, all these structures need to be placed about the garden with the same careful thought you would give to siting topiary or sculpture. Like topiary, you might have plant supports in pairs or singly, positioned throughout the garden; instead of box or yew, you could have a pyramid of jasmine, a column of wisteria or a wigwam of sweet peas.

PUNCTUATION

139

The smallest greenhouse, such as this charming example in a city garden, can entice the gardener to carry on the work of plant propagation on even the coldest and wettest days.

This plain but characterful stone building would have been built using local materials and local labour. The craft of construction and the essential simplicity are inspiration for new buildings in a small garden.

This simple twig and branch structure with its wicker chair offers shelter for one from an occasional shower of rain, or a place to sit and observe wildlife.

Lovely old potting sheds should stay true to their function and contain a supply of pots, clean and ready for use.

This green oak river-hut, with its oak shingle roof, has two closed and two open sides, keeping the hut private and separate from the main garden and, at the same time, reinforcing the strong visual connection to the stream and woodland.

GREENHOUSES AND ORANGERIES, PLEASURE BUILDINGS

A lovely old building with rustic timbers and circular thatched roof has been given a new lease of life by the addition of a fireplace, thus extending the time the building can be enjoyed for relaxation.

This handsome curved greenhouse is the perfect place to grow plants. On a warm midsummer's evening, it could be a magical place to dine.

141

GREENHOUSES AND ORANGERIES

GREENHOUSES ARE FUNCTIONAL BUILDINGS, BUILT expressly for the purpose of propagating plants, but they should, if at all possible, be buildings that are beautiful to look at, as well as to work in. Here, more so than in any other part of the garden, you are in one-to-one contact with plants, handling the seeds and cuttings that will eventually be moved on into the garden. Working in the greenhouse on a rainy day is an experience that most passionate gardeners look forward to, and all the more so if the building is a pleasure to be in.

The kinds of greenhouse that I'm thinking about are the old Victorian brick and timber buildings. You may be fortunate enough to have an old one in the garden, but even if you don't, a good builder or joiner should have no difficulty copying an original or working, perhaps, from a sample section of glazing bar. It is often possible to buy and salvage the timber from old buildings that are no longer in use.

New greenhouses can be built in a variety of ways. There is the free-standing greenhouse that can be sunk into the ground, the lean-to constructed against a wall, or the smaller three-sided structure that can be fitted into a corner. In a small city garden, the greenhouse might be a tiny addition at the back of the house, providing space for a few species pelargoniums; on a shady north wall, it could house a

collection of shade-loving plants, lush ferns, some hoyas for scent or a collection of auriculas.

The original orangeries, or winter gardens, were structures on a grand scale, designed and built to house collections of tender plants and doubling as rooms for entertaining, when the plants were moved outside in summer.

The classic orangery is a room with a solid plastered ceiling and large sash windows facing south, to allow in the maximum amount of light. We can take the essence of these buildings based on historical reference and translate them into a more modest building for our times. The space need not be more than 2.4 x 7m (8 x 23ft). It might have classical Georgian windows, with a small parapet wall hiding a glazed roof with a stone floor. A less expensive structure could be built of breeze blocks, then rendered with lime plaster and limewashed; alternatively it could be given a highly contemporary gloss with the three solid walls in polished concrete and one wall with full-length plate glass windows.

The important thing about these buildings is that they provide an environment separate from the house. Being sheltered, they allow you to extend the hours you spend in the garden; an orangery could be a place to sit and read late into a summer evening or to enjoy the first of the early spring sunshine. Any new building that calls itself an orangery has to be a room for plants – it is all about the smell of compost, leaves and flowers. It is a living, vibrant place that happens to have a roof and large windows to enable the plants to thrive.

PLEASURE BUILDINGS

THE IDEA OF THE GARDEN PAVILION PROBABLY DERIVES from the banqueting houses that were built into the roofscapes of many of the great Elizabethan houses. Guests were taken to the pavilion to eat sweetmeats while admiring the view and the extent of their host's lands. A more recent point of reference is the classical garden temple of the eighteenth-century English landscape garden. These buildings were placed at strategic points in the garden, often near a lake, providing focal points in the vista from the house and offering destinations to visit during your walk or ride around the grounds. Pleasure buildings in today's gardens should have the same purpose, offering a diversion, a shelter from the elements, an end point to

RIGHT This garden pavilion, in its semi-wild, romantic setting, has been designed by Richard Craven using classical proportions. This gives it a human scale that we can relate to, combined with a delightful playfulness.

FAR RIGHT The inspiration for my own garden pavilion came from seventeenth-century engravings by Johannes Kip. The windows and their detailing were copied from the house, to establish a visual link between the two buildings.

a walk. Even the smallest town garden could make space for a little building, perhaps a reading room housing some favourite books providing that it is warm enough in winter to keep the books dry.

Naturally, the placement of any new building within a garden requires thought, and its design and scale should always be in keeping with the size and style of the space. But there is enormous scope for doing something exciting that will add immeasurably to the overall design. Beautiful contemporary structures can be made in a variety of materials and styles, from timber-frame to sculptural rammed-earth constructions. The building might be elevated just high enough above garden level to give you a view over the surrounding countryside. In the eighteenth century, garden pavilions were often built into the corners of garden walls. They would have overlooked the village green or the street, and allowed the owners some connection with the hustle and bustle of the world outside the enclosed environment of the garden. There is a clandestine appeal about being at the edge of a garden and yet elevated slightly out of it, so that you can peer into that other world beyond your walls.

At home, one of my garden buildings looks out onto the sheep field and, in spring, I like to sit and watch the lambs playing on a windy day. Places like this are pure pleasure to be in; time passes and you can lose yourself for hours.

What all these buildings have is a character of their own, something worldly about them that declares: 'This is the kind of building I am.' Whatever the design – whether modern, classical or rustic – the building should be of the best quality

construction and should fit comfortably into the environment. But it must, above all, fulfil the purpose for which it has been made, namely, to provide pleasure and enjoyment. It might be a place to go and read the newspaper, write letters, paint, eat Sunday lunch or have a picnic; there should always be a table and some chairs, maybe a pot-bellied stove or a fireplace.

You might take inspiration from a classical garden building, but reinterpret it in rustic timber with its bark. You could build it yourself and give it a sedum or turf roof, even a tin roof. It might be built of brick or, like mine, be made of breeze block, with a soft lime render and limewash. If the garden is contemporary, then it could be a modern concrete building or be made entirely of glass. If you are working with an existing building in a garden, then it is vital that you make the garden respond sympathetically to that building.

Many Edwardian gardens have picturesque open-sided shelters, often with a built-in seat, that are an integral part of the garden wall. Here, you can sit in the cool on a hot day, or listen to and smell the rain in a sudden summer downpour, at once connected with nature and yet secure and dry. The garden shelter at Peckover House in Wisbech is an excellent example of this simple type of building, and its rusticated oak posts have over the years been covered with layers and layers of high gloss shiny paint, giving it great character. Edwardian summerhouses, unlike our modern flat-pack versions, were designed and built to a very high standard, and were often fixed on a revolving base, so they could be made to face into or away from the sun, according to choice.

It is possible to spend a great deal of money on a garden building, but it is possible to make something delightfully simple for relatively little. For instance, simply by using recycled timber planking for cladding the outside, a couple of old casement windows that have been discarded, and a peg tile or wooden shingle roof, you can make something that is individual, idiosyncratic and totally charming. Another way is to build your structure, either closed- or open-fronted, onto an existing wall.

If you have the inclination, you could make a building out of rammed-earth, digging the soil out of the ground and using only materials that you already have. By building up the earth walls in layers between shuttering, adding some straw in with the mud, trampling the layers down and letting them dry in between, you can make a beautifully sculptural building with fluid lines. You can then render and limewash it. To add further interest, you could make patterns or motifs on the walls of the building with pargeting, which is the art of applying and moulding lime mortar into repeated panels of patterns.

A straw-bale building can be built inexpensively. You would need to build a brick or stone pediment to raise the building out of the soil, then have straw-bale walls on three sides that you cover with lime-plaster. With oak posts at the front and a couple of beams to support a pitched roof of recycled slates or tiles, you've made a lovely building that's environmentally friendly, using only sustainable materials. This type of building is organic and has texture instead of being straight-sided; you could celebrate this by making sinuously curving, even circular or spiralling, walls.

FAR LEFT This contemporary interpretation of a classical rotunda sits very comfortably in its environment, with the slate roof making a perfect link to the colours of the natural rock formation in the distance. The slim stone columns have been left without detailing and blend in easily with the surrounding wild meadow.

ABOVE No longer needed for its original purpose, this old granary has been turned into a wonderful secret retreat. At home, I have turned old outbuildings into, variously, a potting shed, summer dining room and an office.

casework

BELOW LEFT By midsummer
these long grass squares have
changed colour from green to
gold, providing a strong textural
contrast with the mown paths and
changing the face of the garden.

BELOW RIGHT On this gently
sloping site random topiary trees
have been placed like characters
in a play, adding height and form
to an otherwise level site.

This final section takes eight gardens, seven complete and one still at the concept stage, and looks at how their design uses verticals, horizontals and punctuation to create a unified and balanced whole.

In each case, climate and locality provide the gardens with their dominant character. The Mediterranean Terraced Garden, with its vertical rocky setting and hard, brilliant light, has an ambience and colour palette entirely different from that of the Contemporary Country Garden, which is set in the flat agricultural landscape of Normandy, where horizontal lines predominate. While one garden makes repeated use of sculptural forms to counterbalance the effect of the terrain, the other works in close natural harmony with its setting. Visual continuity is also the underlying strength of the Contemporary Formal Garden, the design of which works with the lie of the land around it to create a garden that is powerfully connected to the countryside at all times of year.

The serene Californian Garden has a strongly architectural design, combining a limited colour and planting palette to great effect within a framework of spacious horizontals and well-defined vertical axes. By creating a series of broad, practical terraces and interconnecting garden rooms, the design of the English Country Garden deals elegantly with an awkwardly shaped site and capitalizes on the fine views.

The design of the Small Urban Garden and the City Garden both respond to the built environment by creating a reassuring sense of enclosure with strong vertical lines and punctuation points that amuse and engage. Lastly, the Work in Progress Garden shows the evolution of a design. Work begins with an analysis of the site and the client brief, then draws on observations of locally growing plants and vernacular details, along with inspirational ideas from other sources. It takes its final shape by drawing these influences together in a balanced composition of verticals, horizontals and punctuation.

BELOW The bench in this garden is placed permanently in position, but the small stools double as tables and are moveable, adding a degree of flexibility to the way in which the garden is used.

ABOVE Although recently planted in this position, these olive trees still seem to be rooted in some Arcadian garden. Here, they have been given a new lease of life, though, and their impact is underlined by the parallel lines of lavenders running beneath their ancient boughs.

LEFT These hedges have been clipped into large squares, to reflect the cubic design of the house. Their formal shape adds weight and structure to this part of the terrace, which is closest to the house.

CALIFORNIAN GARDEN

This design by Roger Warner brings ancient and modern together in a successful marriage of style and form. It is the perfect example of a garden where less is more, and where the controlled use of a limited palette of plants, colours and materials has created a space of strength and character. Gnarled and venerable olive trees, planted to form long axes that cross the different horizontal planes, give a strong vertical backbone to the garden. The planting at ground level is in some places structured and formal, elsewhere flowing and naturalistic, but the balance between verticals and horizontals is kept always harmonious.

The soft blue-grey of the olive trees links tonally to the lavender, rosemary and other aromatics, which are set against the tussocks of grass, rounded citrus bushes and wide, flat expanses of lawn. The warm, rich ochre of the building is repeated on the outer boundary walls, drawing the various elements of the garden together and maintaining a powerful unity of site.

A row of citrus trees in pots signals and, at the same time, softens the approach to the house. The neutral colour of the containers harmonizes with the stone chippings of the path.

CASEWORK

LEFT Adjacent to the terrace, a large area of level lawn makes the perfect foil for formally clipped hummocks of lavender and sustains a balance with the formal lines of the house. Further away from the house, the lavenders are allowed to grow more naturally.

RIGHT The pure simplicity of its design means that the pool rests calmly and comfortably within the landscape. The plain stone terrace and understated furniture create no visual boundaries between the garden and its setting.

LEFT The naturalistic style of the planting in this part of the garden, which contrasts strongly with the more formal areas, creates a relaxed feel and encourages the visitor to meander through the plants. Planted close to the house, the citrus perfumes the air with its delicious scent.

ENGLISH COUNTRY GARDEN

I designed and developed this 3-acre garden
has been out of a sloping site into a series of
level and spacious terraces. Each one has been
divided and subdivided into different areas,
which include a rose garden, kitchen garden
and wide herbaceous borders.

As the garden drops away from the house,
the character of the levels changes, becoming
progressively less formal. The third and final
level has an open croquet lawn bordered by
simple estate railings that allow the garden to
dissolve gently into the countryside, while the
second, more formal, terrace comprises two
large lawns, flanked on either side by lavender
gardens enclosed by box hedges. Gaps in the
hedges allow movement in and out of the
different spaces, and broad flights of steps and
paths made from limestone chippings allow
free circulation around the garden.

Adjacent to the house and running along
its length is a York stone terrace. A small knot
garden adds formality and gives the space a
sense of intimacy. The garden has beautiful
vistas over the countryside, with the hedges
separating each terrace left low deliberately to
allow an uninterrupted view of the entire
length of the garden.

LEFT A simple, hand-made
rustic trellis supports a climbing
rose against the barn wall.
Inexpensive details such as this
are beautiful to look at all times
of the year, and very much in
keeping with the character of
the building.

LEFT The first terrace has wide herbaceous borders framing the lawns, with paths of limestone chippings separating them. To one side of the garden there is a woodland; the strong vertical presence of the overhanging trees is counterbalanced by the calm, broad horizontals of the lawns and paths.

BELOW Looking across the first level towards the house and its York stone terrace, the repeating shapes of clipped evergreens punctuate the horizontal plane.

LEFT The house terrace is on a more intimate scale than any of the lower terraces. A 1.5m (5ft) wide box parterre, planted with pale blue iris and clipped standards of elaeagnus, edges the terrace. The formal evergreen shapes help to retain interest during winter.

LEFT The semi-enclosed vegetable garden, containing a greenhouse and raised beds, is entered through a pair of oak gates. This area offers a particularly good vantage point over the garden, so brick walls were built on two sides and one side was left open and bordered simply by a semi-transparent division of oak railings.

RIGHT Keeping an open view across the entire garden was an important element of the design. Looking across the low box hedges into the herbaceous borders on the first terrace, the structure of the garden is apparent, but it never detracts from the garden's beautiful setting.

LEFT Topiary Portuguese laurels (*Prunus lusitanica*) provide another form of textural interest within the rose garden.

ABOVE On an axis with the vegetable garden, the orchard has been designed and planted as an avenue. Halfway along the avenue, the ground rises into a grass mount; at this point the trees change from pip fruits to stone fruits.

LEFT From the columns of
cypress to the box domes in the
foreground, various forms of
clipped shapes within this part of
the garden create a simple and
restful environment. A low stone
slab among the topiary enforces
the strong horizontal emphasis
and adds another layer of texture.

MEDITERRANEAN TERRACED GARDEN

Designed by Nicole de Vesian, this garden in Provence is one of my favourites. With its wealth of textures and scents, it's a hot, musky garden. The terrain is very rocky, but by using plants that thrive in this kind of environment, and by using them well, a wonderful garden has been created. It is made up of a series of levelled terraces that have been carved out of the rock face. Flights of steps brimming with rosemary, box and lavender lead seductively from one area to another. This garden is all about restraint and simplicity but, at the same time, there is terrific depth in the way that it plays with the contrasts in texture and colour, and also how it uses the light to draw out and emphasize these contrasts. Walls of beautifully hewn stone are seen against rougher, more natural walls and the solid rock from which the garden is carved. These strong elements are softened by lovely pockets of calm planting. The restful plant palette is deliberately limited, made up primarily of the blue-greys of lavender with the green of myrtle, box and cypress. There are lavenders that have been allowed to grow and flower planted among lavenders that have been clipped into dense rounded hummocks and mounds. These have become topiaries but, because they are low, they form a lovely, calm horizontal plane.

LEFT At the entrance to the garden, a roughly hewn dry-stone wall is punctuated by a simple stone ball. The entrance is given further emphasis by the cypress tree, which creates a green vertical contrast.

BELOW Water, the life-giver, is especially important in a sun-baked garden. The still, reflective qualities of this pool, carved out of solid rock, invite you to plunge into the cool depths.

LEFT Most of the lavender plants have been allowed to flower, but some are kept close to the ground, underlining the passion for the clipped form within the garden.

BELOW A pair of cypress trees stand sentry at one of the entrances to the garden, providing a necessary visual counterbalance to the door's sturdy construction.

RIGHT This plain wood seat resting on stone blocks is framed to good effect by a stone obelisk on one side and a candelabra pear tree on the other.

RIGHT Sunlight plays an important role in the drama of this garden, adding definition to the shapes of the plants and throwing their precisely clipped forms into sharp relief.

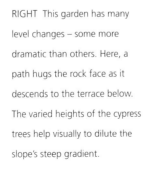

RIGHT This garden has many
level changes – some more
dramatic than others. Here, a
path hugs the rock face as it
descends to the terrace below.
The varied heights of the cypress
trees help visually to dilute the
slope's steep gradient.

163

TOWN GARDEN

This garden design is all about clipped shape and texture, horizontals and verticals. There are no flowers: in summer, it is entirely green, and, in winter, the colour comes from the golden leaves of the beech and the white trunks of the silver birches.

The site is asymmetrical and wedge-shaped, but since the architecture and interior of the house are formal, I wanted to extend this formality into the garden. In addition, large, semi-industrial buildings with corrugated roofs dominated two sides of the garden, so the garden's framework needed to be strong enough to compete with these distractions throughout the year.

The problem of the garden's shape was resolved by creating a rectangular lawn in the middle with a band of limestone chippings around it. The asymmetry is taken up with wedges of beech hedging, straight and parallel to the lawn but triangular at their outer edges. Within this platform of hedging is a serpentine path.

The yew topiaries bordering the lawn provide strong lines in the centre section of the garden, which links in neatly with the formality of the house. To help try and keep costs down, I chose to use limestone chippings instead of stone paving, the surface of which is now acquiring a wonderful patina of moss.

ABOVE Plants have been chosen for their year-round interest. In the winter sun, the white trunks of the silver birches (*Betula utilis* var. *jacquemontii*) look particularly beautiful when seen against the golden leaves of the beech and the dark green yew.

RIGHT Topiary yews running in two rows along the edges of the lawn give the garden a sense of distinction, with a touch of naivety. Each topiary has a different shape – an effective device for giving a quirky, informal twist to a formal design.

BELOW Proportion and the balance of weight are very important in this garden. At the end of the lawn facing the house, a contemporary urn set in a circle of chippings is used as a focal point to stop the eye and divert attention away from the dominant line of the roof behind.

BELOW The serpentine path introduces an important element of fluidity and movement into the garden and also provides views of the house and garden from different angles. The effect of winding in and out of the platform of hedging can be quite disorientating, rather like being in a maze.

RIGHT Throughout the summer, the garden is a tapestry of greens, but with the first frosts, the hornbeam turns a golden yellow, closely followed by the birch and the beech, bringing welcome colour and warmth during the winter months.

BELOW Limestone chippings
make an inexpensive but
attractive surface for a terrace.
In winter, the chippings take on
a cloak of emerald-green moss,
bringing a new shade and texture
to the garden.

BELOW This warm-coloured
old brick wall is the perfect
backdrop to the rich texture
and colour of the dark topiary
yew and the pale stone urn.
It also gives the garden a sense
of security and protection.

CONTEMPORARY FORMAL GARDEN

This design by Tom Stuart-Smith links the garden beautifully to the countryside that surrounds it. It picks up on the scale of the ploughed fields in the background and, merging with them, brings that same scale and sense of spaciousness into the garden. Full use is made, too, of the surrounding mature trees. Their dominant vertical shapes are grounded in the garden by the topiary, the dark green of the upright yews tying in with the cedars and the beech sentinels echoing the beech trees.

The large open plane of water reflects the big skies and brings light into the garden, while the channel of moving water helps to draw the eye into and along the garden. Long parallel lines are repeated throughout the garden with the use of topiary trees and other design elements. There are also informal paths that wind their way through the swathes of naturalistic planting, chosen to look good at all times of the year. In winter, the tall grasses remain upright but they change their character, becoming bleached and flaxen. Together with the golden leaves of the beech, they bring warmth into the garden.

ABOVE At a change in levels, the cascade, with its sheet of flowing water, makes a dramatic punctuation point. It also provides a place to sit and enjoy the sound and sight of the water.

RIGHT The large expanse of still water reflecting the sky creates a strong sense of calm. As the garden is not closed off to the landscape, it needs the weight and density of strong shapes, like the dark, upright yews to define it.

RIGHT Linking the garden to a wooded area, a double row of yews maintains the formality of the rest of the garden and repeats the rhythm of parallel lines. This formation also guides and draws the traveller on towards the boundary.

ABOVE The beech topiary stand
like sentinels, making strongly
vertical points of reference
against the landscape. They
establish a link with the large
mature beech in the distance.
The tree has shed its leaves, but
they retain their juvenile foliage.

LEFT Box hedges create this
big contemporary baroque
brocaded parterre. The contrast
between the low parterre and
the tall grasses adds interest
during the winter months.

BELOW Even in their winter
state, these grasses remain.
In the winter light, the warmth
of the colours contrasts with the
bare outlines of the trees outside
the garden, underlining the
distinction between landscape
and garden.

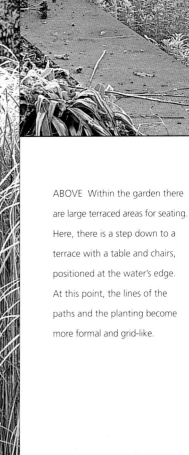

ABOVE Within the garden there
are large terraced areas for seating.
Here, there is a step down to a
terrace with a table and chairs,
positioned at the water's edge.
At this point, the lines of the
paths and the planting become
more formal and grid-like.

SMALL URBAN GARDEN

My design for this small London garden needed to make strong visual connections with both the communal garden at the rear and the contemporary interior design of the house. The main considerations were to create privacy and to give a sense of height, in keeping with the scale of the tall white stucco house.

Privacy was achieved by planting a small enclosure of pleached limes at the centre, which acts as a space for entertaining and forms a 2m (6½ft) high green screen. We recycled the old flagstones, and allowed the paving joints to become filled with mind-your-own-business (*Soleirolia soleirolii*) and, in spring, electric blue scillas. To match the scale of the house and separate the garden from the communal space beyond, large beech topiaries were planted with cubes of yew in between. *Rosa* 'Tuscany Superb' grows out of the paving, and on the walls a simple driftwood trellis is covered with wisteria and roses. Against another wall, a contemporary fountain has been filled with duckweed, introducing a soft country feel that contrasts with the strong urban character of the garden.

BELOW Within the paving joints, mind-your-own-business (*Soleirolia soleirolii*) forms an emerald-green mat. In spring, a mass of scillas grows up through the green, forming an electric blue haze over the surface of the stone.

ABOVE *Rosa* 'Tuscany Superb' has been planted among the borders and within the paving itself, where its richly coloured blooms can spill out onto the hard surface.

LEFT Plain, square terracotta pots are filled with *Pelargonium* 'Lord Bute', mirroring the colour of the roses and maintaining a single colour palette.

LEFT To give additional focus and bring a touch of modernity, the trunks of the lime trees have been limewashed in coloured bands that relate to the contemporary seating in the enclosure.

ABOVE Self-seeding *Alchemilla mollis* colonizes the joints between the stones, adding another texture at ground level, especially after rainfall, when the scalloped leaves hold pearls of water.

RIGHT This bench by Paul
Anderson has a wonderful
sense of playfulness about it
and associates well with the old
York stone paving. It may in time
become a support for some of
the climbers growing nearby.

BELOW Urban and country,
contemporary and traditional,
come together frequently in this
garden. Here, the lime-green of
the duckweed makes a strong
colour contrast with the blue of
the modern ceramic bowl.

175

ABOVE A semi-circle of low hedging sweeps right up to the barn, making a framework to contain the planting. This restraint gives some formality to the area, even though the planting itself is naturalistic.

RIGHT Making patterns within an area of grass is a very effective and inexpensive way of creating formality. This mood is not permanently imprinted on the garden, however: it changes with the seasons as the grass grows long or is cut.

CONTEMPORARY COUNTRY GARDEN

The elegant formality of this garden in Normandy has been created in a naturalistic way by making strong patterns on the horizontal plane using grasses of different heights. The effect is calming and in complete sympathy with the surrounding landscape. The rectangular pool, with its light-reflective surface, is a pure horizontal, and its impact is increased by the large squares of long grass that border it on all four sides.

The mown paths running between the squares of long grass create a pattern of textures that makes connections across the garden and constantly delivers you back to the landscape, focusing the eye on what lies beyond. At the garden boundary, an archway through the outer hedge frames the view of the countryside, bringing it into the garden and drawing you towards it, inviting exploration. The archway, like the wonderful old fruit trees silhouetted against the sky, is an important vertical in a very flat landscape. The garden needs these taller elements to enable it to sit comfortably with the barn. Close to the barn, the garden takes on a greater degree of formality, with smaller areas of box hedging containing flowering plants, making yet more divisions and subdivisions.

ABOVE By borrowing the landscape beyond and bringing it into the garden, the archway in the outer boundary hedge becomes the threshold between two environments. It also introduces much needed height into a flat landscape.

RIGHT Near the house the planting becomes increasingly formal, but the mood is playful, with a pattern of low hedges laid out like a little potager. Gravel replaces grass as the path material, indicating that you have entered a different zone – one that is more 'gardened'.

ABOVE The planting of the perennial plants within the garden are kept simple and thus creates a much bigger impact.

LEFT Naturalistic planting is
contained within a sweep of
low clipped hedging, with little
haystacks making temporary
sculptures on the squares of mown
grass. The garden is full of such
playful reminders of its connections
with the landscape it inhabits.

ABOVE As the summer draws
to a close, the garden is subtly
linked to the countryside and its
practices with small haystacks
built on pyramids of sticks. These
natural sculptures create a form of
punctuation that is organic as well
as simple to make.

CASEWORK

179

1 Swimming pool

9 Corn terrace

2 Kitchen terrace

10 Double hedge walk

3 Courtyard

11 Flax/Fig parterre

4 Herbaceous walk

12 Dovecote

5 Cypress avenue

13 Amphitheatre

6 Pergola

14 Boules court

7 Pleached limes   8 Vine walk

15 Orchard   16 Labyrinth

William Pounds
for Arne Maynard. 2003.

WORK IN PROGRESS
GARDEN

This design project for a garden close to the Pyrenees in France is still at the planning stage. The house sits on a large plot of gently sloping land that extends out into the landscape from the front of the house, with the existing garden just a series of uninviting and disjointed areas. The surrounding arable landscape is powerful but, with no boundary separating it from the garden, it seems quite overwhelming. My aim is to make a series of protective enclosures to lessen this effect and draw people out into the garden, while keeping a connection to the landscape and the fine views.

My first visit to the site was at Easter, when I spent time looking at what was growing in and around the area. I found cercis trees in flower, masses of white and pale blue flag iris, lots of box hedging and pollarded limes, fields of barley, fig trees, a few cypress and herbs, as well as quite a few roses already in flower, tree peonies and lily of the valley. This became my portfolio of plants for the design.

The summers here are baking hot, so I want the design to include shaded areas for relaxation and outdoor dining. By removing the car parking area from the front of the house, the existing entrance courtyard [3] can be transformed into a calm and secluded space, with a fountain and rambling roses scrambling over the walls.

There will be large lawn areas for the children to play on, and a boules court. The garden will also be in tune with the change of seasons in the landscape. With that in mind, the corn terrace [9] will consist of squares of barley that will change from fresh green to flaxen, and then, in autumn, will be cut and stacked in stooks. Later, in winter, the bare ploughed earth will be all that's visible. The more formal upper garden will be divided from this lower 'agricultural' garden by a vine walk [8] that acts as a bridge between the planting styles. Each of these spaces has a connection to the next, and each sets up a series of different routes that, in turn, offer a choice of different experiences. At the furthest edge of the garden, a green amphitheatre [13] will be etched into the slope, from which there will be a magnificent view to the abbey that lies beyond.

RIGHT A pair of oak gates, with espaliered fruit trees positioned on either side, will divide the kitchen terrace [2] from the herb garden. The gates will add a ceremonial element to the entrance.

ABOVE AND BELOW I would like to use pale colours for the flowering plants in the garden. As the summers are so hot and the light is very bright, cooler colours would help to keep the garden looking fresh. Soft pinks and creams, pale blues and mauves would be ideal colours.

LEFT Flag iris are prevalent in this part of France, and I plan to use them in large drifts in the herbaceous borders [4], with clipped box, another widely used plant in the region, forming most of the low hedging.

RIGHT I plan to introduce a range of clipped forms to the garden, including box, bay, yew and rosemary. These clipped yew trees gave me the inspiration for the beginning and end of the vine walk [8].

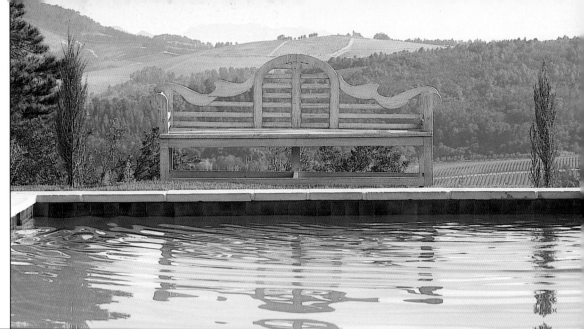

BELOW In my design, I have used two varieties of pleached tree: in the courtyard [3], there is a double row of cercis – a flowering tree often seen locally – and, surrounding the main lawn, pleached limes [7], which will give a sense of seclusion, while allowing views through the trunks to the surrounding countryside.

LEFT The present swimming pool [1] has a bright blue liner, which I would like to change to a neutral stone colour, together with the coping stone around the pool. This will create an altogether softer environment in this part of the garden.

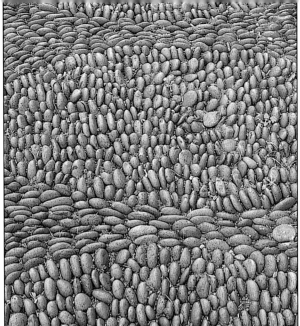

LEFT Around the edge of the kitchen courtyard [3], a drainage channel will be made, laid out as a pebble mosaic. Due to conservation restrictions, the house has no gutters, and this is an attractive vernacular device for dealing with any surplus run-off water.

RIGHT Below the pleached limes [7], adjacent to the swimming pool [1] and running along the house side of the main lawn, a series of clipped box balls and domes will be planted. These will act as a division between the more intimate parts of the garden and the large lawn and garden beyond.

ABOVE A scented garden within the courtyard [3] will include clipped aromatics such as lavender, rosemary and box growing out of the limestone chippings. These structural forms will be interplanted with sages, thymes and agapanthus.

LEFT To provide continuity of colour after the irises have flowered, huge drifts of pale blue agapanthus will be planted in various parts of the garden, such as the herbaceous garden [4], the entrance courtyard [3] and around the swimming pool [1].

BELOW In the courtyard garden
[3], at the centre of the pleached
cercis walk, there will be a
fountain made from local stone.
Here, in this echoing space, the
sound of the water will be given
added resonance.

RIGHT At the end of the vine
walk [8], I am hoping to build
a traditional-style dovecote with
a room in the upper floor. From
here, there will be a view of the
corn fields beyond and also onto
the corn terrace [9] at the outer
edge of the garden.